>>>>>> >>>>>>>> >>>>>>>

THE GOSPEL OF TRUTH

The Mystical Gospel

>>>>>> >>>>>>>> >>>>>>>

THE GOSPEL OF TRUTH

The Mystical Gospel

by Mark M. Mattison

Also by Mark M. Mattison

The Gospel of Mary:
A Fresh Translation and Holistic Approach

The Gospel of Judas:
The Sarcastic Gospel

The Gospel of Thomas:
A New Translation for Spiritual Seekers

The Gospel of Q:
Jesus' Prophetic Wisdom

The Gospel of Philip:
The Divine Mysteries of Marriage and Rebirth

The Gospel of Peter:
Revisiting Jesus' Death and Resurrection

For more information, visit:
http://www.gospels.net

First Edition

© 2018 Mark M. Mattison. All rights reserved.

Scripture quotations marked DFV are from the *Divine Feminine Version* (DFV) of the New Testament, made publicly available through the Creative Commons License – Attribution, Noncommercial, Share Alike 3.0 United States. For full details see:
http://creativecommons.org/licenses/by-nc-sa/3.0/us

Scripture quotations marked NRSV are from the New Revised Standard Version Bible, Copyright © 1989 by the Division of Christian Education of the National Council of the Churches in Christ in the United States of America.

Scripture quotations marked NIV are from the HOLY BIBLE, NEW INTERNATIONAL VERSION, Copyright © 1973, 1978, 1984 International Bible Society. Used by permission of Zondervan Bible Publishers.

Contents

Acknowledgements	8
Introduction	9
1: The Core Teachings of the Gospel of Truth	12
2: The Gospel of Truth: A New Translation	27
3: Valentinus and His Followers	42
Appendix A: The Gospel of Truth: A Public Domain Translation	47
Appendix B: Two Versions of the Gospel of Truth	65
Notes	68
Bibliography	78

The Gospel of Truth: The Mystical Gospel

Acknowledgements

I'd like to express my gratitude to all the women and men of the Grand Rapids Writer's Exchange who have played such an important role in my journey as a writer over the last eleven years. Their constructive criticism of my writing has been invaluable.

Thanks are specifically due to Justin Reamer and Wes Thompson for reviewing the manuscript. I'm also indebted to Dr. Lance Jenott for providing additional bibliographical references and helping me to work through a difficult passage or two in the Coptic, and particularly to Dr. Samuel Zinner for taking the time to help me work through a number of interpretative issues. Of course, I remain solely responsible for any errors or mistakes.

Finally, I'm deeply grateful to my wife, Rebecca, whose graceful and patient encouragement is a source of inexhaustible spiritual strength.

The Gospel of Truth: The Mystical Gospel

Introduction

Scholars have long known about ancient Gospels that weren't included alongside the New Testament's famous four (Matthew, Mark, Luke, and John). Until recently, however, most of these Gospels were known only by reputation. Some ancient theologians named and described them, but didn't preserve them for posterity. Some, like the Gospel of Thomas, they quoted. Others, like the Gospel of Judas, they derided. But astonishing archaeological finds have turned them up – many just over the last century.

That's also the story of the Gospel of Truth. Described late in the second century by Irenaeus of Lyons (*Adv. Haer.* III.11.9), it remained lost to history until the discovery of a dozen leather-bound Coptic (Egyptian) books near the village of Nag Hammadi in 1945. Many of these fourth-century Egyptian texts are translations of earlier Greek texts dating as early as the second century, including the Gospel of Truth. It was among the first of the Nag Hammadi texts scholars translated.[1]

Actually, two copies of the Gospel of Truth were found in the Nag Hammadi library: a nearly complete version in the first volume, and a few fragments of a second version in the twelfth volume. The translations presented in this book are based on the more complete copy in the first volume.

What makes this Gospel unique? First, it doesn't present a narrative storyline (like Matthew, Mark, Luke, John, Mary, Judas, or Peter), nor a list of Jesus' sayings (like Thomas or Q). Consequently, it's more like the Gospel of Philip, a collection of spiritual reflections. In fact, many believe it's rather a sermon *about* the Gospel. Along those lines, Bentley Layton has described the Gospel of Truth as "the earliest surviving sermon of Christian mysticism."[2] As a mystical reflection on the meaning of the Gospel, this text provides us another rare glimpse into the lives of some of Jesus' followers before their movement became a powerful institutional church.

Who wrote this unusual text? According to Irenaeus, followers of Valentinus used "the Gospel of Truth," and many of its terms and ideas do seem consistent with how Irenaeus and others described the teaching of Valentinus and his followers. However, it lacks some of the more detailed doctrines that they attributed to Valentinus and his followers.[3] We should also note that this text doesn't actually bear its title, unlike many other Gospels (cf. Mary, Judas, Thomas, and Philip). Its identification with the text described by Irenaeus depends partly on its contents, and partly on its opening words: "The Gospel of Truth is a joy ...."[4]

From the beginning, scholars have concluded that Valentinus himself wrote the text,[5] and many still maintain that view.[6] It closely resembles surviving fragments of Valentinus' writings that have been preserved by the "church fathers," and its poetic beauty seems consistent with Valentinus' legendary talent and genius.[7] Although later scribes probably revised this Gospel extensively in the light of later theological controversies (see Appendix B), it remains plausible that Valentinus wrote the original version.

Who was Valentinus? Born at the beginning of the second century in Egypt, he started teaching in Alexandria probably sometime between 117 and 138 CE.[8] According to another second-century Christian, Clement of Alexandria, many claimed Valentinus was a disciple of Theudas, who in turn was a disciple of Paul.[9] Sometime between 136 and 140 CE, Valentinus moved to Rome,[10] where his talents nearly led to his becoming bishop. Even his opponents grudgingly admired his rhetorical skill; Tertullian wrote that "Valentinus had expected to become a bishop, because he was an able man both in genius and eloquence."[11] However, followers of Jesus in Rome were deeply divided during the second century. In the midst of conflict,

The Gospel of Truth: The Mystical Gospel

Valentinus withdrew from the acrimony, content to teach those who were willing to listen.[12] And many did: several renowned second-century teachers followed in the tradition of Valentinus, as we'll discuss in Chapter Three.

If Valentinus did write the Gospel of Truth, his reputation as an eloquent teacher was well-deserved. This powerful text seamlessly blends New Testament scriptures with Greek philosophy and Hellenistic Judaism to create deeply compelling images. But what do all these poetic images mean, and what are the core teachings of the Gospel of Truth?

The Gospel of Truth: The Mystical Gospel

1
The Core Teachings of the Gospel of Truth

Understanding the Gospel of Truth can be challenging, especially since it lacks a chronological narrative. Harold W. Attridge and George W. MacRae write that part of what makes it "particularly difficult is that the text operates at the same time on a number of different levels, using symbolic language which has a multiplicity of referents."[1] Though some interpretations should remain tentative, we may draw some plausible conclusions by considering its relationship with other texts, as well as internal clues.

The Gospel of Truth and Other Scriptures

Arguably, the Gospel of Truth makes much sense in the context of John's Gospel, especially chapter 17 (which focuses on the theme of unity) and John's prologue.[2] For example, six key terms in John 1:1-18 ("Father," "Word," "fullness," "grace," "truth," and "know") are all found in the very first sentence of the Gospel of Truth:

> The Gospel of *Truth* is a joy for those who've received *grace* from the *Father* of *Truth,* that they might *know* him through the power of the *Word* that came from the *fullness* – the one who's in the thought and mind of the *Father* (Gospel of Truth, page 16, public domain translation, emphasis mine).

The author also shows intimate familiarity with many other New Testament texts, including Matthew, Romans, Ephesians, Philippians, Colossians, 2 Corinthians, 2 Timothy, Hebrews,

12

The Gospel of Truth: The Mystical Gospel

James, 2 Peter, 1 John, and Revelation. Few scholars have noted direct allusions to the Jewish Bible; for example, in his marginal references, Bentley Layton cites only Genesis among all the Hebrew scriptures. It may be tempting to conclude from this that the author was far removed from the world of Judaism. However, at several points the Gospel of Truth shows considerable familiarity with Semitic thought.

One example is its teaching about "repentance." The Greek word for "repentance" simply means "a change of mind."[3] But in the Gospel of Truth, "repentance" implies more than simply change; it means a "return" (page 35), which is also what it meant in Rabbinic Hebrew.[4]

Another example is the recurring subject of "the name."

"The Name" in the Gospel of Truth

The Gospel of Truth discusses "the name" on pages 21, 22, 27, and 38 through 41. The first set of references (pages 21, 22, and 27) refer to God "naming" God's children generally, but in the latter portion of the text (pages 38 through 41), it functions as a key concept to explain the relationship between God "the Father" and "the Son." The most well-known passage, on page 38, states:

> Now the name of the Father is the Son. He's the one who first gave a name to the one who comes out from him, who was himself, and he gave birth to him as a Son. He gave him his name which belonged to him. He's the one to whom everything around the Father belongs. The name and the Son are his. It's possible for him to be seen; the name, however, is invisible, because it alone is the mystery of the invisible which comes to ears that are filled completely with it by him. For indeed, the Father's name isn't spoken, but it's revealed through a Son (public domain translation).

The Gospel of Truth: The Mystical Gospel

Why so much emphasis on "the name"? What is "the name" of God? Kendrick Grobel writes that it's probably "no specific name, in our sense, such as 'Jahweh' or 'Lord' or 'God,' but name in a deeper, ultimately Hebraic sense: essential nature."[5] Similarly, Attridge and MacRae write:

> Here, as Grobel (*Gospel*, 183) notes, we find the most explicit reference to the Jewish tradition of the *Shem hammephorash*. Cf. 38.11-12. The fact that the Father's name is not spoken serves as the image for the transcendence of the Father's essence.[6]

What these scholars are describing is the ancient Jewish practice of not pronouncing the name of God, which in Hebrew is represented by four consonants, YHWH, known as "the Tetragrammaton." Elliot Wolfson elaborates at greater length:

> The Hebraic background [is] enhanced by the reference to the ineffable name, which, as a number of scholars have noted, brings to mind the Jewish conception of the *shem ha-meforash*. The doctrine of the Son bearing the name of the Father, an idea whose roots stretch back to Second Temple Jewish reflections on the Tetragrammaton and the theophanic figures enclothed thereby, is a central motif in early Christology, attested in several books of the New Testament (John 17:11; Rev 19:12-13, 16; Heb 1:4; Rom 10:13; Phil 2:9; Eph 1:21).[7]

If in fact the "name" christology of the Gospel of Truth is grounded in Jewish tradition, it could highlight a little-recognized "bridge" between Semitic thought and fourth-century Christian tradition about "the Son" sharing the same "essence" as the Father. It also could demonstrate that the Gospel of Truth is closer to other Christian traditions than many have thought (cf. Chapter Three).

In addition, we can note the similarity between the Gospel of Truth and more familiar works written by other second-century theologians (known as "the Apologists"). For example, both describe "the Word" as "coming out" from God. According to the Gospel of Truth, "the Word ... was the first to come out" (p. 37, public domain version). Similarly, Theophilus of Antioch writes that "God, then, having [God's] own Word internal within [God's] own bowels, begat him, emitting him along with [God's] own wisdom before all things" (*Autol.* 2.10; cf. 2.22; Athenagoras, *Supplic.* 10).[8]

We may note also that the Gospel of Truth reflects the consensus view that "the Word" was incarnated (embodied; cf. pages 23, 26) in "Jesus Christ." But what of the others who "are named" and "come out" from God? How do they relate to the Word?

"The All" in the Gospel of Truth

Throughout the Gospel of Truth, we read about "all" who "came out" from God. Is this "all" a technical term referring only to certain divine beings who emerge from God, as described by the "church fathers" commenting on Valentinian theology? Or is it a more general term describing all living beings (including humans), as in "every being"? Many scholars suggest the latter,[9] and this conclusion makes very good sense of the text. Whereas "all" are initially "within" God and subsequently "come out" from God, "the Word" was the first to "come out" (page 37), becoming "a Way" (pages 18, 31) showing "all" how to return to God. (On the question of "universalism," see below.) "All" are spiritually birthed when they're "named." That's when they awake from their illusions and ignorance (pages 29, 30, 33), and become aware of who they are and to whom they're destined to return.

When are they "named"? When Jesus is crucified. According to the Gospel of Truth, Jesus "put on" the "living Book of the Living" (page 20), which can't be taken by anyone except the one who's "to be killed." The reference to Revelation 5:3 is clear. In turn, the "living Book of the Living" contains the names of "all" (page 21),[10] and it's published like a "will" (page 20; cf. Heb. 9:17) when Jesus is "nailed to a tree." This passage clearly echoes Ephesians 2:15, 16 and Colossians 2:14, with a key difference: in Ephesians and Colossians, Jesus' crucifixion abolishes the Torah, whereas in the Gospel of Truth, the publication of God's "edict" on the cross doesn't imply a negation of Torah. On the contrary, this passage may also be read in light of texts like Baruch 3:37 – 4:1, in which God's Wisdom is personified precisely in the Torah:

> Afterward she [Wisdom] appeared on earth
> And lived with humankind.
> She is the book of the commandments of God,
> The law that endures forever.
> All who hold her fast will live,
> And those who forsake her will die (*The Inclusive Bible*).

If Hellenistic Jewish texts like this influenced the Gospel of Truth, the implication would be that in "putting on" the "living Book of the Living," Jesus puts on the Torah, that is, the embodiment of God's Wisdom.[11] When he "publishes" this book in his death on the cross[12] (and becomes "the fruit of the Father's knowledge" – note that in rabbinic tradition, Torah is described as fruit "of supernal wisdom"[13]), that's when those who are "named" in the book receive a spiritual birth. That's when they "come out" from the unknowable divine presence, receive their names, and understand from whom they came and to whom they are to return through "the Way" – that is, Jesus.

The Divine Mother

The connection between Jesus and Lady Wisdom / Torah, however, is not the only divine feminine imagery we encounter in the Gospel of Truth. Admittedly, divine feminine imagery isn't nearly as prevalent as divine masculine imagery; the word "Father" as a description of God occurs 87 times, whereas the word "Mother" appears only twice, as a description of Jesus (pages 24 and 42).[14]

The Gospel of Truth: The Mystical Gospel

The image of Jesus as a nurturing (even breastfeeding) Mother is prefigured, among other New Testament texts, in 1 Peter 2:2, 3:

> As newborn babies, long for the pure spiritual milk, so that by it you may grow into life if you've tasted that the Lord is gracious (DFV).

However, this imagery resonates even stronger with the Odes of Solomon,[15] a second-century Syrian text, in which breast milk is described with the language of "sweetness":

A cup of milk was offered to me,
   And I drank it in the sweetness of the joy of the Lord.
The cup is the Son,
   The Father is the one who has been milked,
   And the holy Spirit milked him.
Because his breasts had become full,
   And it was not desired that his milk would be released without purpose.
The holy Spirit opened her chest [bosom],
   And mixed the milk of the two breasts of the Father.
She gave the mixture to the generation when they were ignorant,
   And the ones who received it, they are in the perfection of the Right Hand
(Odes of Solomon 19:1-5, *A New New Testament*).

Compare this text to the following passages in the Gospel of Truth:

> In this way, the Word of the Father goes out in all, as the fruit [of] his heart and an expression of his will. ... returning them to the Father and to the *Mother*, Jesus of infinite *sweetness*.

The Father reveals his *bosom*, and his *bosom* is the Holy Spirit (Gospel of Truth 23, 24, public domain translation, emphasis mine; cf. also page 42).

When the light spoke through his mouth, and by his voice gave birth to life, he gave them thought, wisdom, mercy, salvation, and the Spirit of power from the infinity and *sweetness* of the Father (Gospel of Truth 31, public domain translation, emphasis mine).

... and to glorify the fullness, the greatness of his name, and the Father's *sweetness* (Gospel of Truth 41, public domain translation, emphasis mine).

Feminine imagery in the Gospel of Truth, however, is not limited to the divine. There is another feminine image with a darker side: the image of Error.

Who, or What, is Error?

Immediately following the first paragraph (which, as we've noted above, is grounded in John 1:1-18), the author introduces "Error." The meaning of "Error" here has been the subject of some debate.[16] The translations in this book use a neuter pronoun to describe Error, but in the Coptic language, there is no neuter gender, and the word for "Error" is actually feminine.

When Error first appears on page 17, it seems like a mythological being; Error "was strengthened" and created its own work. Elsewhere Error becomes "angry" at Jesus (page 18) and "anxious" (page 26). Many scholars see here a description of the creator god ("demiurge"), conceived as a lower divine being who fashions the material creation. Some early followers of Jesus not only believed that a "demiurge" created the world, but that this demiurge was ignorant (at best) or evil (at worst).[17] Jörgen Magnusson writes that: "Few if any would oppose the view that the notion of a demiurge figure has coloured the way in which Error is depicted."[18] But even if a mythological demiurge has *influenced* the image of Error here, does it fully *explain* it? Does the

The Gospel of Truth: The Mystical Gospel

Gospel of Truth understand Error simplistically as a malevolent divine being? Several clues suggest that it does not.

For example, Error may be "strengthened," "angry," and "anxious," but it also "has no root" (page 17) and "is empty, with nothing inside it" (page 26). It does not truly exist.[19] Furthermore, although Error pursues Jesus on page 18, notice how seamlessly the pronoun turns from singular to plural:

> Error was angry. *It* pursued him. *It* was threatened by him and brought to nothing. *They* nailed (Jesus) to a tree (emphasis mine).

Commenting on this passage, Magnusson writes that probably, "Error is simultaneously a symbolic designation for the group of people that persecuted Jesus and a description of their mental state." He goes on to write:

> To sum up, Error is strongly coloured by an unusually evil demiurge figure. The characteristics of the demiurge spread over to a group of people who carries out deeds that are driven by false knowledge, fear and anger. In a deeper sense, however, Error does not really exist. It is nothing, and focusing on it only helps it to prevail. The Father's children are therefore much better off if they only pay attention to the Father.[20]

There is, however, another likely source for the figure of Error in the Gospel of Truth. As discussed above, Error is introduced immediately after the Gospel's prologue, which in turn is rooted in John 1:1-18. In John's Gospel, "the Word" which "was in the beginning" (John 1:2) and "became flesh" (John 1:14) was heavily influenced by Lady Wisdom in Jewish literature. For example, consider the following excerpt from Proverbs:

> I, Wisdom, am the habitat of sound judgment,
> the source of clear thinking.
> YHWH gave birth to me at the beginning,
> before the first acts of creation.
> I have been from everlasting,
> in the beginning, before the world began.
> For you who find me find life,
> And earn the favor of YHWH
> (Proverbs 8:12, 22, 23, 35, *The Inclusive Bible*).

Why is this significant? Because Proverbs also introduces a counterpart to Lady Wisdom, described as Lady Folly:

> Folly is an unruly woman;
> > she is simple and knows nothing
> (Proverbs 9:13, NIV).

Drawing these threads together, Samuel Zinner puts it succinctly:

> To sum up my views on the Gospel of Truth: I think John 1 and 17 play a fundamental role throughout. John 1's creation concern allows the author to go back to Gen 1:1-3, and he imports into it the Prov 8-9 tropes of personified Wisdom and Error. I believe this is how the author came to the idea of how evil arises in creation – in imitation of Lady Wisdom's traditional role in creation, he read Lady Folly / Error back into the creation narrative as well.[21]

Rest in Paradise

Magnusson proposes another point of contrast between Error and Truth, based on the following text from page 18:

> They nailed (Jesus) to a tree, and he became the fruit of the Father's knowledge. However, (the fruit) didn't cause destruction when it was eaten, but those who ate it rejoiced

in the discovery. He discovered them in himself, and they discovered him in themselves.

This passage portrays the cross as the Tree of Life, in contrast with the Tree of the Knowledge of Good and Evil described in Genesis 3. Unlike the fruit of the tree which brought death, the fruit of the cross / Tree of Life brings knowledge of the Father (and those who eat it discover Christ in themselves, a reference to the Eucharist). Magnusson writes that the "imagery with two trees also brings to mind the thought of two gardeners," the Father being "the good and perfect gardener who takes care of the paradise with all its fruits" and "Error as an evil and imperfect gardener."[22]

On page 36 of the Gospel of Truth, we read of the Father:

> He's good. He knows his plants, because he planted them in his paradise. Now his paradise is a place of rest.

This image of the Father's paradise is also deeply influenced by the Odes of Solomon.[23] For example, Ode 11 states:

> And I ran in the path, in his peace,
>   In the way of Truth.
> From the beginning and until the end
>   I received his knowledge.
> I was established upon the rock of Truth,
>   Where he set me.
> And from above he restored me without blemish,
> I was as the earth which is sprouting and lush in her fruits.
> My breath was made sweet
>   in the sweet fragrance of the Lord.
> He brought me into his paradise,
> In which is the store of the lusciousness [The same root as "sweetness"] of the Lord.
> I saw trees that were ripe and bearing fruit.
> (Odes of Solomon 11:3b-5, 12, 15-16a, *A New New Testament*.)

The Gospel of Truth: The Mystical Gospel

The Questions of Predestination and Universalism

Above we discussed "all" as a more general term describing all living beings (including humans). For contemporary readers, this naturally raises questions about predestination and universalism in the Gospel of Truth. If "all" are to return to God, doesn't that imply universalism – that "all" will be "saved"? Karen King answers in the affirmative: "it can be argued that, according to *GosTruth*, all of humanity will be saved."[24]

Whereas universalism may be an ideal in the Gospel of Truth, however, like other ancient writers, the author seems resigned to the possibility that some may not be saved in the end. The only rational explanation seems to be that like Error, they, too, must be delusions; but the author also holds out some hope for them in the statement that "the one who's ignorant *until the end* is a delusion of forgetfulness, and they'll dissolve with it (forgetfulness)" (page 21, emphasis mine). The qualifying phrase "until the end" underscores the fact that for many ancient writers, human fate was not necessarily as firmly fixed as it may sound to contemporary readers. People may be predisposed to certain fates, even strongly so; but in practical terms, ancient philosophers and theologians often recognized the capacity of human agents to change.

Of course, that principle can work both ways. In fact, this may explain the Gospel of Truth's famous parable of the jars, which has also been the subject of some debate. Here's the core of the passage:

> It's like some who've left their home, having jars that weren't any good in places. They broke them, but the master of the house doesn't suffer any loss. Instead he rejoices, because in place of the bad jars are ones that are full and complete. For this is the judgment that's come from above; it's judged everyone. It's a drawn, two-edged sword which cuts both ways. The Word, which is in the hearts of those

who speak it, appeared. It isn't just a sound, but it was incarnated (embodied).

A great disturbance arose among the jars, because some were empty, others filled; some provided for, others poured out; some purified, others broken. All the realms were shaken and disturbed, because they didn't have order or stability (pages 25 and 26, public domain translation).

Whom do the "jars" represent, and what does the parable describe? Scholars naturally look to key New Testament passages for clues. For example, Grobel finds the source of this passage in Romans 9:20-24,[25] which symbolically describes some people as "vessels of wrath," compared to others who are "vessels of mercy." On the other hand, Magnusson argues that 2 Timothy 2:15-26 provides a more specific context.[26] This passage reads in part:

A large house has not only gold and silver vessels, but wood and clay vessels too. Some are for special use and others are for ordinary use. So anyone who cleanses themself from these things will be a vessel for special use (2 Tim. 2:20, 21a, DFV).

The context of this image is strife and division within the community; the author even singles out specific transgressors by name (v. 17). Those who stir up controversy are inferior vessels, but those who "avoid empty chatter" (v. 16) are more valuable. The vessels or jars, then, would primarily represent the community of Jesus' followers. A key passage on page 36 in the Gospel of Truth provides support for this interpretation:

"Seek, and those who were disturbed will receive a return – and he'll anoint them with ointment." The ointment is the mercy of the Father, who will have mercy on them. But those whom he anointed are those who have been completed, because full jars are the ones that are anointed. But when the anointing of one dissolves, it empties, and the cause of the need is the place where the ointment leaks, because a breath and its power draws it. But from the one who has no need, no seal is removed, nor is anything emptied, but what it needs is filled again by the Father, who's complete (public domain translation).

So, vessels or jars are "anointed" with oil (chrismated), part of an ancient ritual associated with becoming a follower of Christ.[27] However, these jars can leak, leading to judgment. Page 26 describes this judgment as "a drawn, two-edged sword which cuts both ways," invoking the language of Hebrews 4:12.[28] But is this judgment certain? The paragraph immediately preceding the parable of the jars describes a process of purification "from multiplicity into Unity" (page 25), which would appear to be available to *all* the jars in the ensuing parable.

On the other hand, if the parable of the jars is part of a mystical tradition common to both Judaism and Christianity, another parallel may be considered in Lurianic Kabbalah: the Shattering of the Vessels. In this tradition, God's emanations are like vessels which are unable to fully contain the light of divine consciousness. As a result, they're shattered, scattering sparks of divine light throughout all of creation. Rabbi David A. Cooper writes:

> Every particle in our physical universe, every structure and every being, is a shell that contains sparks of holiness. Our task, according to Luria, is to release each spark from the shell and raise it up, ultimately to return it to its original state. The way these sparks are raised is through acts of lovingkindness, of being in harmony with the universe, and through higher awareness.[29]

The Shattering of the Vessels does sound much like the "great disturbance" which "arose among the jars," leading to instability and Error which in turn is reversed by the coming of Truth (page

26).[30] This could explain the author's confidence that "If indeed these things have happened to each one of us, then it's right for us to think about all, so that this house will be holy and silent for the Unity" (page 25).

Though complex in its imagery and deeply layered in its poetic rhetoric, the Gospel of Truth is simple in its core message: All come from God and will ultimately return to God. Ignorance and Error distract us with frightening illusions, but when we disregard Error and turn to the divine, we come to the spiritual rest of completion, like plants flourishing in God's paradise.

Notes on Translation

Readers who are familiar with my previous translations will know that, as far as possible, I try to avoid using masculine language for God[31] – partly because God is not literally "male," and partly because Christians have historically described God in exclusively male language, to the detriment of many women who feel alienated by this lack of inclusive language. However, I haven't avoided masculine language about God in these translations, for two reasons. First, avoiding gendered language about God has proven too challenging with the pronouns of many passages; and, second, the Gospel of Truth also uses divine feminine language (although not to the same degree). Consequently, I've essentially retained the original text's masculine and feminine language of the divine, although I have tried to mitigate the impact of masculine generic language elsewhere (as in my use of the "singular they," now widely accepted, to address the lack of an inclusive third-person singular pronoun in English).

The Coptic text of the Gospel of Truth also uses pronouns so frequently that it can be difficult to know exactly to whom or what those pronouns refer. The problem is compounded by the fact that there is no neuter gender in Coptic. This results in some ambiguities that have dogged translators from the beginning. Where I believe the referents of the pronouns are clear, I've included subjects in parentheses. In the translation of Chapter Two, I've occasionally even replaced pronouns by subjects entirely, again in parentheses. Words in parentheses are not part of the original text, but are included for editorial clarification.

In addition, these translations use square brackets. These indicate gaps (known as "lacunae") in the manuscript. Words in square brackets are hypothetical reconstructions (educated guesses) based on the size of the gap, the number of letters that probably would have fit in that gap, and the surrounding context. Bold numbers interspersed throughout represent page numbers of the original manuscript. Bold section headings are not found in the Coptic, but are provided for ease of reference. This fact should be kept in mind, since dividing the text in this way is itself an act of interpretation.

2
The Gospel of Truth: A New Translation

Prologue

16 The Gospel of Truth is a joy for those who've received grace from the Father of Truth, so that they might know him through the power of the Word that came from the fullness. The Word is in the thought and mind of the Father. They call him "Savior." That's the name of the work he'll do to redeem those who had become **17** ignorant of the Father. And the term "the Gospel" is the revelation of hope, the discovery of those who search for him.

Error and Forgetfulness

All searched for the one from whom they had come. All were within him, the uncontainable, inconceivable one who's beyond every thought. Ignorance of the Father caused anguish and terror, and the anguish grew thick like a fog, so that no one could see. As a result, Error was strengthened. It worked on its own matter in vain, not knowing the Truth.

It happened in a deluding way, as (Error) prepared in power and beauty a substitute for the Truth. Now this wasn't humiliating for the uncontainable, inconceivable one, because the anguish, forgetfulness, and delusion of deceit were like nothing, whereas the Truth is established, unchangeable, unperturbed, and beyond beauty. Because of this, disregard Error, since it has no root.

It happened (then) in a fog concerning the Father. It happens (now) since (Error) prepares works in forgetfulness and terror, so that with them (Error) might attract and imprison those who are in the middle.

The forgetfulness of Error wasn't revealed; it wasn't a **18** [thought] from the Father. Forgetfulness didn't come from the Father, though it did come because of him. What comes into being in him is knowledge, which was revealed so that forgetfulness might end, and the Father might be known. Forgetfulness came because the Father was unknown, so when the Father comes to be known, forgetfulness won't exist anymore.

The Gospel

This is the Gospel of the one they search for, revealed to those who are complete through the mercies of the Father, the hidden mystery. Through (the Gospel), Jesus Christ enlightened those who were in darkness through forgetfulness. He enlightened them. He showed them a Way, and the Way is the Truth (cf. John 14:6) which he taught them.

As a result, Error was angry. It pursued him. It was threatened by him and brought to nothing. They nailed (Jesus) to a tree, and he became the fruit of the Father's knowledge. However, (the fruit) didn't cause destruction when it was eaten, but those who ate it rejoiced in the discovery. He discovered them in himself, and they discovered him in themselves.

All are within the uncontainable, inconceivable one, the Father, the complete one who made all, and all need him. Although he kept their completion within himself which he didn't give to all, the Father wasn't jealous. Indeed, how could there be jealousy between him and his members? **19** For if, like this, the generation [received the completion,] they couldn't have come […] the Father. He keeps their completion within himself, giving it to them so they can return to him with a unitary knowledge in completion. He's the one who made all. All are within him, and all need him.

The Gospel of Truth: The Mystical Gospel

Like someone who's unknown, he wants to be known and loved — because what did all need if not the knowledge of the Father?

(Jesus) became a guide, peaceful and leisurely. He came and spoke the Word as a teacher in places of learning. Those who thought they were wise came up him to test him, but he confounded them because they were vain. They hated him because they weren't really wise. After they came, all the little children came too; they know the Father. When they were strengthened, they were taught about the Father's expressions. They knew and they were known; they received glory and they gave glory. In their hearts the living Book of the Living was revealed, which was written in the thought and mind **20** [of the] Father, and before the [foundation] of all (cf. Rev. 13:8) within his incomprehensibility. It's impossible to take this (book), since the one who takes it is to be killed (cf. Rev. 5:3). No one could've been revealed among those who'd been entrusted with salvation unless the book had appeared. Because of this, the merciful and faithful Jesus patiently suffered (cf. Heb. 2:17, 18) until he took that book, since he knows that his death is life for many (cf. Matt. 20:28).

When a will hasn't yet been opened, the wealth of the deceased master of the house is hidden (cf. Heb. 9:17); so too all were hidden while the Father of all was invisible. They were from him, from whom every realm comes. Because of this:

> Jesus was revealed,
> put on that book,
> was nailed to a tree,
> and published the Father's edict on the cross (cf. Col. 2:14).

Oh, what a great teaching!

> Drawing himself down to death (cf. Phil. 2:8),
> he clothed himself in eternal life (cf. 1 Cor. 15:53),
> stripped himself of the perishable rags,

The Gospel of Truth: The Mystical Gospel

and clothed himself in incorruptibility,
which no one can take from him.

When he entered the empty realms of terror, he passed through those who were stripped by forgetfulness. He was knowledge and completion, proclaiming the things that are in the heart **21** [...] teach those who will [receive teaching].

The Book of the Living

Now those who will receive teaching [are] the living who are written in the Book of the Living. They receive teaching about themselves from the Father, and return to him again.

Since the completion of all is in the Father, it's necessary for all to go up to him. Then, if someone knows, they receive what belongs to them, and he draws them to himself, because the one who's ignorant is in need. And it's a great need, since they need what will complete them. Since all can find completion only in the Father, it's necessary for all to go up to him, and for each one to receive what belongs to them. He wrote these things beforehand, having prepared them to give to those who came from him.

Those whose names he knew beforehand were called (cf. Rom. 8:29) at the end, so that the one who knows is the one whose name the Father has called, because those whose name hasn't been spoken are ignorant. Indeed, how can someone hear if their name hasn't been called? For the one who's ignorant until the end is a delusion of forgetfulness, and they'll come to their end along with (forgetfulness). Otherwise, why do these miserable ones have no **22** name? Why do they have no voice?

So if someone knows, they're from above (cf. John 3:3). If they're called, they hear, they reply, and they turn to the one who calls them. They go up to him, and they know how they're called. Having knowledge, they do the will of the one who called them. They want to please him, and they receive rest. Each one's name becomes their own. The one who knows like this knows where they come from and where they're going. They know like someone who, having been drunk, turns from their drunkenness, and having returned to themselves, restores what belongs to them.

He's returned many from Error. He went before them to the realms from which they had moved away. They had received Error because of the depth of the one who surrounds every realm, though nothing surrounds him. It's amazing that they were in the Father, not knowing him, and that they were able to come out by themselves, since they weren't able to grasp and know the one in whom they were. He revealed his will as knowledge in harmony with all that came from him.

This is the knowledge of the living book which he revealed to the **23** generations at the end, letters from him revealing how they're not vowels or consonants, so that one might read them and think they're meaningless. Instead, they're letters of the Truth – they speak and know themselves. Each letter is a complete thought, like a book that's complete, since they're letters written by the Unity. The Father wrote them so that by means of his letters, the generations might know him.

The Return to Unity

His Wisdom meditates on the Word,
his teaching speaks it,
his knowledge has revealed it,
his patience is a crown upon it,
his joy is in harmony with it,
his glory has exalted it,
his image has revealed it,
his rest has received it,
his love made a body around it,
his faith embraced it.

In this way, the Father's Word goes out in all, as the fruit **24** [of] his heart and an expression of his will. But it supports all. It chooses them and also takes the expression of all, purifying them and returning them to the Father and to the Mother, Jesus of infinite sweetness.

The Father reveals his bosom (cf. John 1:18), and his bosom is the Holy Spirit. He reveals his hidden self, which is his Son, so that through the Father's mercies the generations may know him and stop searching for him, resting in him and knowing that this is rest. He's filled the need and ended its appearance. Its appearance is the world in which it served, because where there's envy and strife there's need, but where there's Unity there's completion. Since need came into being because the Father wasn't known, once the Father is known, need won't exist anymore. As someone's ignorance ends when they gain knowledge, and as darkness ends when the light appears, **25** so also need ends in completion. So the appearance is revealed from then on, but it'll end in the harmony of Unity.

For now, their works lie scattered. In time, Unity will complete the realms. Within Unity each one will receive themselves, and within knowledge they'll purify themselves from multiplicity into Unity, consuming matter within themselves like fire, and darkness by light, death by life (cf. 2 Cor. 5:4). If indeed these things have happened to each one of us, then it's right for us to think about all, so that this house will be holy and silent for the Unity.

The Parable of the Jars

It's like some who've left their home, having jars that weren't any good in places. They broke them, but the master of the house doesn't suffer any loss. Instead he rejoices, because in place of the bad jars are ones that are full and complete. For this is **26** the judgment that's come from above. It's judged everyone (cf. John 3:19). It's a drawn, two-edged sword (cf. Heb. 4:12) which cuts both ways. The Word appeared, which is in the hearts of those who speak it. It isn't just a sound, but it was incarnated (embodied; cf. John 1:14).

The Gospel of Truth: The Mystical Gospel

A great disturbance arose among the jars, because some were empty, others filled; some provided for, others poured out; some purified, others broken. All the realms were shaken and disturbed, because they didn't have order or stability. Error was anxious. It didn't know what to do; it grieved, mourned, and hurt itself, because it knew nothing. The knowledge, which is (Error's) destruction, approached (Error) and all that came from it. Error is empty, with nothing inside it.

Truth came into their midst, and all that came out knew it. They welcomed the Father in Truth with a complete power that joins them with the Father. Truth is the Father's mouth; the Holy Spirit is his tongue. Everyone who loves the Truth and are joined to the **27** Truth are joined to the Father's mouth. By his tongue they'll receive the Holy Spirit. This is the revelation of the Father and his manifestation to his generations. He revealed what was hidden of himself. He explained it, because who has anything, if not the Father alone?

Coming into Being

Every realm comes out from him. They know they've come out from him like children who are from someone who's completely mature. They knew they hadn't yet received form or a name. The Father gives birth to each one (cf. Jas. 1:19). Then, when they receive form from his knowledge, although they're really within him, they don't know him. But the Father is complete (cf. Matt. 5:48), knowing every realm that's within him. If he wants to, he reveals whomever he wants, giving them a form and a name. He gives them a name, and causes those to come into being who, before they come into being, are ignorant of the one who made them.

I'm not saying, then, that those who haven't yet come into being are nothing, but they exist **28** in the one who will want them to come into being when he wants, like a later time. Before everything is revealed, he knows what he'll produce. But the fruit which he hasn't yet revealed doesn't yet know anything, nor does it do anything. In addition, every realm which is itself in the Father is from the one who exists, who establishes them from what doesn't exist. For those who have no root have no fruit either. They think to themselves, "I've come into being," but they'll end by themselves. Because of this, those who didn't exist at all won't (ever) exist.

The Parable of the Nightmares

Then what did he want them to think of themselves? He wanted to them to think, "I've come into being like the shadows and phantoms of the night." When the light shines on the terror which they received, they know that it's nothing. In this way, they were ignorant of the Father, whom **29** they didn't see. Since it was terror, disturbance, instability, doubt, and division, many illusions were at work among them, as well as vain ignorance, like they were deep in sleep and found themselves in nightmares.

Either they're running somewhere, or unable to run away from someone; or they're fighting, or being fought; or they're falling, or flying through the air without wings. Sometimes, too, it's like someone is killing them, even though no one's chasing them; or they themselves are killing those around them, covered in their blood. Until those who are going through all these nightmares can wake up, they see nothing, because these things are nothing.

That's the way it is with those who've cast off ignorance like sleep. They don't regard it as anything, nor do they regard its **30** other works as real, but they abandon them like a dream in the night. They value the knowledge of the Father like they value the light. The ignorant have acted like they're asleep; those who've come to knowledge have acted like they've awakened.

Good for the one who returns and awakens! Blessed is the one who's opened the eyes of those who can't see! The Holy Spirit hurried after them to revive them. Having given a hand to the one who lay on the ground, it set them up on their feet, because they hadn't yet arisen. It gave them the knowledge of the

Father and the revelation of the Son, because when they saw him and heard him (cf. 1 John 1:1), he granted them to taste him and to grasp the beloved Son.

The Revelation of the Son

When he was revealed, he taught them about the Father, the uncontainable one, and breathed into them what's in the thought, doing his will (cf. John 6:38). When many had received the light, they turned **31** to him. For the material ones were strangers, who didn't see his form or know him. For he came by means of fleshly form (cf. Rom. 8:3), and nothing could block his path, because incorruptibility can't be grasped. Moreover, he said new things while he spoke about what's in the Father's heart, and brought out the complete Word. When the light spoke through his mouth, and by his voice gave birth to life, he gave them thought, wisdom, mercy, salvation, and the Spirit of power from the infinity and sweetness of the Father. He caused punishments and torments to cease, because they led astray into Error and bondage those who needed mercy. He stopped them, and confounded them with knowledge. He became:

> a Way (cf. John 14:6) for those who were led astray,
> knowledge for those who were ignorant,
> a discovery for those who were searching,
> strength for those who were wavering, and
> purity for those who were impure.

The Parable of the Sheep

He's the shepherd who left behind the ninety- **32** nine sheep which weren't lost. He went and searched for the one which was lost (cf. Matt. 18:12). He rejoiced when he found it, because ninety-nine is a number expressed with the left hand. However, when the one is found, the numerical sum moves to the right hand. In this way, the whole right hand, which needs the one, draws what it needs from the left hand and moves it to the right, so the number becomes one hundred. This is a symbol of the sound of these numbers. This is the Father.

Even on the Sabbath, he worked for the sheep which he found fallen in the pit (cf. Matt. 12:11). He saved the life of the sheep, having brought it up from the pit, so that you may know in your hearts – you're children of the knowledge of the heart – what is the Sabbath, on which it isn't right for salvation to be idle, so that you may speak of the day which is above, which has no night, and of the light that doesn't set, because it's complete. Speak then from the heart, because you're the completed day, and the light that doesn't cease dwells (cf. Rev. 21:25) within you. Speak Truth with those who search for it, knowledge with those who've sinned in their Error.

Doing the Father's Will

33 Strengthen the feet of those who stumble, and reach out to those who are sick (cf. Matt. 10:8). Feed those who are hungry (cf. Matt. 25:25), and give rest to those who are weary (cf. Matt. 11:28). Raise up those who want to arise (cf. Matt. 10:8), and awaken those who sleep, because you're the understanding that's unsheathed. If strength is like this, it becomes stronger.

Be concerned about yourselves. Don't be concerned about other things which you've rejected. Don't return to eat your vomit (cf. 2 Pet. 2:22). Don't be eaten by worms (cf. Matt. 6:19), because you've already shaken it off. Don't become a dwelling-place for the devil (cf. Eph. 4:27), because you've already brought it to naught. Don't strengthen your obstacles which are collapsing, as though you're a support. For the lawless one is nothing, to be treated more harshly than the just, doing his works among others.

So do the Father's will, because you're from him. For the Father is sweet, and goodness is in his will. He knows what's yours, that you may find rest in them. For by the fruits they know what's yours (cf. Matt. 7:16, 20), because the children of the Father **34** are his fragrance (cf. 2 Cor. 2:14), since they're from the grace of his expression. Because of this, the Father loves his fragrance, and reveals it everywhere. And when it mixes with matter, it gives his fragrance to the light, and in tranquility he causes it to rise above every form and every sound. For it's not the ears that smell the fragrance, but it's the Spirit that smells, and draws the fragrance to itself, and sinks down into the Father's fragrance. Then he shelters it, and takes it to the place from which it came, from the first fragrance which has grown cold. It's something in a soul-endowed delusion, like cold water sunk into loose earth. Those who see it think that it's just earth. Afterwards, it evaporates. If a breath draws it, it becomes warm.

So the fragrances which are cold are from the division. Because of this, faith came. It ended the division, and brought the fullness that's warm with love, so that the cold may not return, but rather the unitary thought of completion.

Restoring what was Needed

This is the Word of the Gospel of the discovery of the fullness, which comes for those who are awaiting **35** the salvation which is coming from above. The hope for which they're waiting is waiting for those whose image is light with no shadow in it (cf. 1 John 1:5). If at that time the fullness comes, the need of matter doesn't come through the infinity of the Father, who comes to give time to the need – although no one can say that the incorruptible one will come like this. But Father's depth multiplied, and the thought of Error didn't exist with him. It's something that's fallen, which is easily set upright in the discovery of the one who's to come to what he'll return, because the return is called "repentance."

Because of this, incorruptibility breathed out. It followed after the one who sinned, so that they might rest, because forgiveness is what remains for the light in need, the Word of fullness. For the doctor hurries to the place where there's sickness, because that's what (the doctor) wants to do. The one in need, then, doesn't hide it, because (the doctor) has what they need. In this way the fullness, which has no need but fills the need, is what he **36** provided from himself to fill up what's needed, so that they might receive grace; because when they were in need, they didn't have grace. Because of this, a diminishing took place where there's no grace. When what was diminished was restored, what they needed was revealed as fullness. This is the discovery of the light of Truth which enlightened them, because it doesn't change.

Because of this, they spoke of Christ in their midst: "Seek (cf. Matt. 7:7), and those who were disturbed will receive a return. He'll anoint them with ointment (cf. 1 John 2:27)." The ointment is the Father's mercy. He'll have mercy on them. But those whom he anointed are those who've been completed, because full jars are the ones that are anointed. But when the anointing of one dissolves, it empties, and the cause of the need is the place where the ointment leaks, because a breath and its power draws it. But from the one who has no need, no seal is removed, nor is anything emptied; but what it needs is filled again by the Father, who's complete.

The Father's Paradise

He's good. He knows his plants, because he planted them in his paradise. Now his paradise is a place of rest. This **37** is the completion in the Father's thought, and these are the words of his meditation. Each of his words is the work of his one will in the revelation of his Word. When they were still in the depths of his thought, the Word – which was the first to come out – revealed them along with a mind that speaks the one Word in a silent grace. He was called "the Thought," since they were in it before being revealed. So it happened that he was the first to come out at the time when it pleased the one who wanted it. Now the Father rests in his will, and is pleased with it.

Nothing happens without him, nor does anything happen without the will of the Father, but his will is incomprehensible (cf. Matt. 10:29). His trace is the will, and no one can know him, nor does he exist for people to scrutinize so that they might grasp him, but when he wills, what he wills is this – even if the sight doesn't please them in any way before God – the will of the Father, because he knows the beginning of all of them, and their end, for in the end he'll greet them directly. Now the end is receiving knowledge of the one who's hidden; this is the Father, **38** from whom the beginning has come, and to whom all who've come out will return. They were revealed for the glory and the joy of his name.

The Father's Name

Now the name of the Father is the Son. He's the one who first gave a name to the one who comes out from him, who was himself, and he gave birth to him as a Son (cf. Heb. 1:5). He gave him his name which belonged to him (cf. John 17:11). He's the one to whom everything around the Father belongs. The name and the Son are his. It's possible for him to be seen; the name, however, is invisible, because it alone is the mystery of the invisible which comes to ears that are filled completely with it by him. For the Father's name isn't spoken, but it's revealed through a Son.

In this way, then, the name is great. So who will be able to utter a name for him, the great name, except him alone to whom the name belongs, and the children of the name – those in whom the Father's name rests, and who themselves, in turn, rest in his name? Since the Father is unbegotten, it's he alone who gave birth to him for himself as a name, before he had made the generations, so that the Father's name might be over their head as Lord, which is the **39** true name, confirmed in his command in complete power. For the name isn't from words and naming. The name, rather, is invisible.

He gave a name to him alone. He alone sees him, he alone having the power to give him a name, because whoever doesn't exist has no name. For what name will they give one who doesn't exist? But the one who exists, exists also with his name, and he alone knows it. He's given a name to him alone. This is the Father; his name is the Son. So he didn't hide it within, but it existed. The Son alone gave a name. So the name belongs to the Father, as the name of the Father is the beloved Son. Where, indeed, would he find a name, except from the Father?

But doubtless one will ask their neighbor, "Who is it who'll give a name to the one who existed before them, as if **40** offspring didn't receive a name from those who gave them birth?" First, then, it's right for us to consider what the name is. It's the true name, the name from the Father, because it's the proper name. So he didn't receive the name on loan, the way others do, according to the form in which each one will be produced. So this is the proper name. No one else gave it to him. But he's unnameable, indescribable, until the time when the one who's complete spoke of him alone. And he has the power to speak his name and see him.

So when it pleased him that his beloved name should be his Son, and he gave the name to him who came out from the depth, he disclosed his secrets, knowing that the Father is without evil. Because of this, he brought him out so that he might speak about the place, and his resting place from which he'd come, **41** and to glorify the fullness, the greatness of his name, and the Father's sweetness.

The Place of Rest

Each one will speak about the place from which they came, and they'll hurry to return again to the place where they received their restoration to receive from the place where they were, receiving a taste from that place and receiving nourishment, receiving growth.

And their place of rest is their fullness. So all that have come from the Father are fullnesses, and the roots of all that have come from him are within the one who caused them all to grow. He gave them their destinies. Then each one was revealed, so that through their own thought [...] for the place to which they send their thought is their root, which takes them up through all the heights, up to the Father. They embrace his head, which is rest for them, and they're grasped, approaching him, as though to say that they receive his expression by means of kisses. But they're not revealed **42** in this way, because they neither exalted themselves, nor wanted the Father's glory. Nor did they think of him as trivial, harsh, or wrathful; but he's without evil, unperturbed, and sweet. He knows every realm before they've come into existence, and he has no need to be instructed.

This is the way of those who possess something of the immeasurable greatness from above, as they wait for the complete one alone, who's a Mother for them. And they don't go down to Hades. Nor do they have envy or groaning, nor death within them (cf. Rev. 21:4), but they rest in the one who rests – not striving or twisting around in the search for Truth. But they themselves are the Truth, and the Father is within them, and they're in the Father, being complete. They're undivided from the truly good one. They don't need anything, but they rest, refreshed in the Spirit. And they'll listen to their root. They'll devote themselves to those things that they'll find in their root and not suffer loss to their soul. This is the place of the blessed; this is their place.

Conclusion

As for the others, then, may they know, where they're at, that it's not right **43** for me, having come to the place of rest, to say anything more. I'll come to be in (the rest), and will devote myself continually to the Father of all and the true brothers (and sisters) – those upon whom the Father's love is emptied (cf. Rom. 5:5) and in whose midst there is no need. They're the ones who are revealed in Truth. They exist in the true eternal life, and they speak of the light that's complete and that's filled with the Father, and that's in his heart and in the fullness. His Spirit rejoices in it, and glorifies the one in whom it existed, because he's good. And his children are complete, and worthy of his name, because he's the Father. It's children like this that he loves.

3
Valentinus and His Followers

As noted in the Introduction, many scholars believe Valentinus authored the original Greek version of the Gospel of Truth. Though the "church fathers" preserved only fragments of his original writings, Valentinus made a deep and lasting impression, much to the chagrin of those who castigated him as a dangerous "heretic."

Irenaeus of Lyons wrote the earliest historical records about Valentinus. Irenaeus composed his five-volume *Against Heresies* sometime around 180 CE. In the preface to his work, he explains that he based his criticism on direct conversations with some of "the disciples of Valentinus."[1] According to Irenaeus, Valentinus "adapted the principles of the heresy called 'Gnostic' to the peculiar character of his own school."[2]

In recent years, scholars have debated both of these claims: first, that Valentinus was a "Gnostic" (or at least influenced by a "heresy called Gnostic"); and, second, that Valentinus' disciples were part of a philosophical "school" as opposed to part of the developing church community.

Was Valentinianism "Gnostic"?

"Gnosticism" is a more recent term scholars have used to categorize a "heresy" described by ancient "heresiologists" of the church, including Irenaeus, Hippolytus of Rome, Tertullian of Carthage, and Epiphanius of Salamis.[3] Until the middle of the twentieth century, these "church fathers" remained the primary historical sources for this apparently loose collection of movements.

The Gospel of Truth: The Mystical Gospel

This more recent label, "Gnosticism," was inspired by the ancient label "Gnostic," from the Greek word *gnōsis*, which means "knowledge." Irenaeus himself based his work on 1 Timothy 6:20, which warns against "the empty chatter and opposing ideas of so-called knowledge *(gnōseōs)*."[4] But although Irenaeus describes something "called Gnostic," no one he wrote about ever referred to *themselves* as "Gnostic," as if that label denoted a specific movement or group of movements.

Though the heresiologists spilled much ink describing what "Gnostics" believed, scholars building on their work tried to define ancient "Gnosticism" by summarizing key principles stemming from a dualistic view of spirit and matter – spirit being inherently good and matter being inherently evil.[5] If God is spiritual (good), then who could have created a physical universe (evil)? Apparently, a "demiurge" or "craftsman," a divine being lower than the true God. As described in Chapter One, this "demiurge" must have been ignorant (at best) or evil (at worst). This "demiurge" would then have enslaved good spirits in the prison of human bodies. How, then, could these good spirits escape their evil physical bodies and ascend to heaven? By receiving the teaching of the spiritual Christ, who could not have been truly human and so could not have died on the cross or risen from the dead, as traditional Christianity has maintained. The practical ramifications of these teachings, it was thought, led to one of two extremes: either an "ascetic" ethic that all material pleasure is also evil, or a "libertine" ethic that since matter is evil anyway, whatever spiritual people do in the flesh is irrelevant.

The discovery of the Nag Hammadi Library in Egypt in 1945 expanded the available source material for these movements. Scholars now had direct access to many of the texts these so-called "Gnostics" wrote and used. At first, they read these texts in light of what the heresiologists wrote. But more recently, some have questioned these traditional readings.[6] They point out that the Nag Hammadi texts don't all represent the same viewpoint, and furthermore that none of them individually contains all the teachings described above.[7] Several don't even contain any of them.

In short, many question that something called "Gnosticism" ever existed outside the creative imaginations of the heresiologists and church historians.

The Gospel of Truth itself provides an excellent test case. Is this text "Gnostic," or an example of "Valentinian Gnosticism"? Given the broad definition of "Gnosticism" above, the Gospel of Truth appears to fail that test on all counts. Karen King writes:

> *GosTruth*, a writing from the mid-second century thought by many scholars to have been written by "the arch-heretic" Valentinus himself, is an excellent example of a work that defies classification as a "Gnostic" text. This remarkable work exhibits none of the typological traits of Gnosticism. That is, it draws no distinction between the true God and the creator, for the Father of Truth is the source of all that exists. It avows only one ultimate principle of existence, the Father of Truth, who encompasses everything that exists. The Christology is not docetic; Jesus appears as a historical figure who taught, suffered, and died. Nor do we find either a strictly ascetic or a strictly libertine ethic; rather, the text reveals a pragmatic morality of compassion and justice.[8]

Was Valentinianism a Philosophical "School"?

If they weren't "Valentinian Gnostics," how should we understand Valentinus and his followers?[9] This question leads to the second of Irenaeus' foundational claims, that Valentinianism was a philosophical "school" as opposed to a legitimate part of Jesus' movement in the second century.

But there seems to be little support for this allegation, either. How could Valentinus have almost become bishop of Rome if he weren't part of the developing church? Granted, Valentinus and teachers following in his tradition were educated, but that need not imply that they were any less part of the nascent church than other educated teachers.[10]

Some argue that the following text from the Gospel of Truth describes Valentinianism as a philosophical school:

> (Jesus) became a guide, peaceful and leisurely. He came and spoke the Word as a teacher in places of learning (page 19).

Instead of "places of learning," Grobel uses the word "a school,"[11] Attridge and MacRae use the word "schools,"[12] and Layton uses "classrooms."[13] By contrast, Meyer uses "places of instruction,"[14] and *A New New Testament* uses "places of learning."[15] Geoffrey S. Smith writes:

> The term rendered "schools" by Attridge and MacRae ... literally means "places of learning" and likely refers to the Jerusalem temple, local synagogues, and less formal venues where Jesus taught, such as mountainsides, lakeshores, and private residences. ... Thus there is no evidence in independent Valentinian sources to suggest that they conceived of themselves as members of a school. In contrast, when Valentinians do discuss their own identity, they consistently employ ecclesiastical language.[16]

Though the writings of their opponents may remain our most reliable sources (to date) for information about the lives and careers of Valentinus and the teachers who carried on (or developed) his tradition,[17] one should read their accounts with a critical eye.

Irenaeus, Tertullian, and the other heresiologists were hardly dispassionate observers. Their sarcastic language and rhetorical strategies invite caution. The polemical strategies they use have often proved effective in political and social conflicts. Critics lump together people and groups who have little in common, describe them with labels that they don't (or wouldn't) use of themselves, and describe their beliefs or ideas in the least flattering light. The heresiologists used these strategies so well that only recently have scholars started to disentangle and question their categories.

Read on their own terms, many of these ancient Gospels defy traditional criticisms. The way we frame them is critical. If we assume they're "heretical" before we even read them, we're likely to find exactly what we expect to find. But if we read them the way we read other early texts written by Jesus' followers – that is, letting them speak for themselves – we tend to find very different things. As discussed in Chapter One, the core message of the Gospel of Truth is spiritually profound. We all come from God, who loves us, and we return to God through Jesus' "Way."

The Gospel of Truth: The Mystical Gospel

Appendix A:
A Public Domain Version of the Gospel of Truth

The translation in this appendix has been committed to the public domain. It may be freely copied and used, in whole or in part, changed or unchanged, for any purpose.

The text is based on NHC I, *3* – that is, the third tractate of the first volume of the Nag Hammadi Codices, a library of ancient Egyptian texts dating to the fourth century. Apart from some fragments in the last codex (book), it's the only surviving copy of this text to date. It begins on page 16, line 31, and ends on page 43, line 24. Scholars widely agree that it's a translation of an earlier Greek manuscript, and that the text was initially composed in the second century.

Though not titled, this text opens with the words, "The Gospel of Truth is a joy for those who've received grace…." According to the second-century bishop Irenaeus of Lyons, the followers of Valentinus used a Gospel that they referred to as "the Gospel of Truth." It's not possible to know for certain that Irenaeus was referring to this text, but it clearly reflects Valentinian theology. Many have argued that Valentinus himself wrote it.

The translation of this appendix is intended to be a more literal translation than that of Chapter Two. In both translations, however, there are some gaps (known as "lacunae") in the manuscript that are denoted by square brackets. Words in square brackets are hypothetical reconstructions (educated guesses) based on the size of the gap, the number of letters that probably would have fit in that gap, and the surrounding context. Words in parentheses are strictly editorial additions to clarify the meaning of the text. Bold numbers throughout the text denote the manuscript's page numbers (beginning with page 16). Bold section headings are not found in the original Coptic, but are provided for ease of reference. This fact should be kept in mind, since dividing the text in this way is itself an act of interpretation. A series of text notes at the end provide additional information on translation choices, including comparisons with previous translations of the Gospel of Truth.

Prologue

16 The Gospel of Truth is a joy for those who've received grace from the Father of Truth, that they might know him through the power of the Word that came from the fullness – the one who's in the thought and mind of the Father. They call him "Savior." That's the name of the work he'll do to redeem those who had become **17** ignorant of the Father. And the term "the Gospel" is the revelation of hope, the discovery of those who search for him.

Error and Forgetfulness

Since all searched for the one from whom they had come – all were within him, the uncontainable, inconceivable one who's beyond every thought – (and) since ignorance of the Father caused anguish and terror, and the anguish grew thick like a fog, so that no one could see – Error was strengthened. It worked on its own matter in vain, not knowing the Truth.

It happened in a deluding way, as it (Error) prepared with power, in beauty, a substitute for the Truth. Now this wasn't humiliating for the uncontainable, inconceivable one, because the anguish and forgetfulness and delusion of deceit were like nothing, whereas the Truth is established, unchangeable, unperturbed, beyond beauty. Because of this, disregard Error, since it has no root.

It happened in a fog concerning the Father. It happens (now) since it (Error) prepares works in forgetfulness and terror, so that

The Gospel of Truth: The Mystical Gospel

with them it (Error) might attract those in the middle and imprison them.

The forgetfulness of Error wasn't revealed; it wasn't a **18** [thought] from the Father. Forgetfulness didn't come into being from the Father, though it did come into being because of him. What comes into being within him is the knowledge, which was revealed so that forgetfulness might be dissolved, and the Father might be known. Forgetfulness came into being because the Father was unknown, so when the Father comes to be known, forgetfulness won't exist anymore.

The Gospel

This is the Gospel of the one they search for, revealed to those who are complete through the mercies of the Father, the hidden mystery. Through it (the Gospel), Jesus Christ enlightened those who were in darkness through forgetfulness. He enlightened them; he showed them a Way, and the Way is the Truth which he taught them.

As a result, Error was angry. It pursued him. It was threatened by him and brought to nothing. They nailed him (Jesus) to a tree, and he became the fruit of the Father's knowledge. However, it (the fruit) didn't cause destruction when it was eaten, but those who ate it were given joy in the discovery. He discovered them in himself and they discovered him in themselves.

As for the uncontainable, inconceivable one – the Father, the complete one who made all – all are within him, and all need him. Although he kept their completion within himself which he didn't give to all, the Father wasn't jealous. Indeed, what jealousy is there between him and his members? **19** For if, like this, the generation [received the completion,] they couldn't have come […] the Father. He keeps their completion within himself, giving it to them to return to him with a unitary knowledge in completion. He's the one who made all, and all are within him, and all need him.

49

The Gospel of Truth: The Mystical Gospel

Like someone who's unknown, he wants to be known and loved — because what did all need if not the knowledge of the Father?

He became a guide, peaceful and leisurely. He came and spoke the Word as a teacher in places of learning. Those who were wise in their own estimation came up to him to test him, but he confounded them because they were vain. They hated him because they weren't wise in Truth. After all of them, all the little children came too; theirs is the knowledge of the Father. When they were strengthened, they received teaching about the Father's expressions. They knew and they were known; they received glory and they gave glory. In their hearts the living Book of the Living was revealed, which was written in the thought and mind **20** [of the] Father, and before the [foundation] of all within his incomprehensibility. This (book) is impossible to take, since it permits the one who takes it to be killed. No one could've been revealed among those who'd been entrusted with salvation unless the book had appeared. Because of this, the merciful and faithful Jesus patiently suffered until he took that book, since he knows that his death is life for many.

When a will hasn't yet been opened, the wealth of the deceased master of the house is hidden; so too all were hidden while the Father of all was invisible. They were from him, from whom every realm comes. Because of this:

> Jesus was revealed,
> put on that book,
> was nailed to a tree,
> and published the Father's edict on the cross.

Oh, what a great teaching!

> Drawing himself down to death,
> he clothed himself in eternal life,
> stripped himself of the perishable rags,

and clothed himself in incorruptibility,
which no one can take from him.

When he entered the empty realms of terror, he passed through those who were stripped by forgetfulness, being knowledge and completion, proclaiming the things that are in the heart **21** [...] teach those who will [receive teaching].

The Book of the Living

Now those who will receive teaching [are] the living who are written in the Book of the Living. They receive teaching about themselves, and they receive it from the Father, returning to him again.

Since the completion of all is in the Father, it's necessary for all to go up to him. Then, if someone has knowledge, they receive what are their own, and he draws them to himself, because the one who's ignorant is in need. And it's a great need, since they need what will complete them. Since the completion of all is in the Father, it's necessary for all to go up to him, and for each one to receive what are their own. He inscribed these things beforehand, having prepared them to give to those who came out from him.

Those whose names he knew beforehand were called at the end, so that the one who has knowledge is the one whose name the Father has called, because those whose name hasn't been spoken are ignorant. Indeed, how can someone hear if their name hasn't been called? For the one who's ignorant until the end is a delusion of forgetfulness, and they'll dissolve with it. Otherwise, why do these miserable ones have no **22** name? Why do they have no voice?

So if someone has knowledge, they're from above. If they're called, they hear, they reply, and they turn to the one who calls them. And they go up to him, and they know how they are called. Having knowledge, they do the will of the one who called them, they want to please him, and they receive rest. Each one's name becomes their own. The one who has knowledge like this knows where they come from and where they're going. They know like one who, having been drunk, turns from their drunkenness, and having returned to themselves, restores what are their own.

He's returned many from Error. He went before them to the realms from which they had moved away. They had received Error because of the depth of the one who surrounds every realm, though nothing surrounds him. It's a great wonder that they were in the Father, not knowing him, and that they were able to come out by themselves, since they weren't able to grasp and know the one in whom they were. He revealed his will as knowledge in harmony with all that emanated from him.

This is the knowledge of the living book which he revealed to the **23** generations at the end, letters from him revealing how they're not vowels or consonants, so that one might read them and think they're meaningless, but they're letters of the Truth – they speak and know themselves. Each letter is a complete thought, like a book that's complete, since they're letters written by the Unity, the Father having written them so that the generations, by means of his letters, might know the Father.

The Return to Unity

> His Wisdom meditates on the Word,
> his teaching speaks it,
> his knowledge has revealed it,
> his patience is a crown upon it,
> his joy is in harmony with it,
> his glory has exalted it,
> his image has revealed it,
> his rest has received it,
> his love made a body around it,
> his faith embraced it.

In this way, the Word of the Father goes out in all, as the fruit **24** [of] his heart and an expression of his will. But it supports all.

The Gospel of Truth: The Mystical Gospel

It chooses them and also takes the expression of all, purifying them, returning them to the Father and to the Mother, Jesus of infinite sweetness.

The Father reveals his bosom, and his bosom is the Holy Spirit. He reveals what's hidden of himself; what's hidden of himself is his Son – so that through the mercies of the Father, the generations may know him and cease their work in searching for the Father, resting in him and knowing that this is the rest. He's filled the need and dissolved its appearance – its appearance is the world in which it served, because where there's envy and strife there's need, but where there's Unity there's completion. Since need came into being because the Father wasn't known, when the Father is known, from then on, need will no longer exist. As someone's ignorance dissolves when they gain knowledge, and as darkness dissolves when the light appears, **25** so also need dissolves in completion. So the appearance is revealed from then on, but it'll dissolve in the harmony of Unity.

For now, their works lie scattered. In time, Unity will complete the realms. Within Unity each one will receive themselves, and within knowledge they'll purify themselves from multiplicity into Unity, consuming matter within themselves like fire, and darkness by light, death by life. If indeed these things have happened to each one of us, then it's right for us to think about all, so that this house will be holy and silent for the Unity.

The Parable of the Jars

It's like some who've left their home, having jars that weren't any good in places. They broke them, but the master of the house doesn't suffer any loss. Instead he rejoices, because in place of the bad jars are ones that are full and complete. For this is **26** the judgment that's come from above; it's judged everyone. It's a drawn, two-edged sword which cuts both ways. The Word, which is in the hearts of those who speak it, appeared. It isn't just a sound, but it was incarnated (embodied).

A great disturbance arose among the jars, because some were empty, others filled; some provided for, others poured out; some purified, others broken. All the realms were shaken and disturbed, because they didn't have order or stability. Error was anxious. It didn't know what to do; it grieved, mourned, and hurt itself, because it knew nothing. The knowledge, which is its (Error's) destruction, approached it (Error) and all that emanated from it. Error is empty, with nothing inside it.

Truth came into their midst, and all that emanated knew it. They welcomed the Father in Truth with a complete power that joins them with the Father. Truth is the Father's mouth; the Holy Spirit is his tongue. Everyone who loves the Truth and are joined to the **27** Truth are joined to the Father's mouth. By his tongue they'll receive the Holy Spirit. This is the revelation of the Father and his manifestation to his generations. He revealed what was hidden of himself; he explained it, because who has anything, if not the Father alone?

Coming into Being

Every realm emanates from him. They know they've come out from him like children who are from someone who's completely mature. They knew they hadn't yet received form or a name. The Father gives birth to each one. Then, when they receive form from his knowledge, although they're really within him, they don't know him. But the Father is complete, knowing every realm that's within him. If he wants to, he reveals whomever he wants, giving them a form and a name. He gives a name to them, and causes those to come into being who, before they come into being, are ignorant of the one who made them.

I'm not saying, then, that those who haven't yet come into being are nothing, but they exist **28** in the one who will want them to come into being when he wants, like a later time. Before everything is revealed, he knows what he'll produce. But the fruit which he hasn't yet revealed doesn't yet know anything, nor does it do anything. In addition, every realm which is itself in the Father is from the one who exists, who establishes them from what doesn't exist. For those who have no root have no fruit either. They think to themselves, "I've come into being," but they'll dissolve by themselves. Because of this, those who didn't exist at all won't exist.

The Parable of the Nightmares

What, then, did he want them to think of themselves? He wanted to them to think, "I've come into being like the shadows and phantoms of the night." When the light shines on the terror which they received, they know that it's nothing. In this way, they were ignorant of the Father, whom **29** they didn't see. Since it was terror and disturbance and instability and doubt and division, many illusions were at work among them, and vain ignorance, like they were deep in sleep and found themselves in nightmares. Either they're running somewhere, or unable to run away from someone; or they're fighting, or being beaten; or they've fallen from heights, or fly through the air without wings. Sometimes, too, it's like someone is killing them, even though no one's chasing them; or they themselves are killing those around them, covered in their blood. Until those who are going through all these nightmares can wake up, they see nothing, because these things are nothing.

That's the way it is with those who've cast off ignorance like sleep. They don't regard it as anything, nor do they regard its **30** other works as real, but they abandon them like a dream in the night. They value the knowledge of the Father like they value the light. The ignorant have acted like they're asleep; those who've come to knowledge have acted like they've awakened. Good for the one who returns and awakens! Blessed is the one who's opened the eyes of those who can't see! The Holy Spirit hurried after them to revive them. Having given a hand to the one who lay on the ground, it set them up on their feet, because they hadn't yet arisen. It gave them the knowledge of the Father and the revelation of the Son, because when they saw him and heard him, he granted them to taste him and to grasp the beloved Son.

The Revelation of the Son

When he was revealed, he taught them about the Father, the uncontainable one, and breathed into them what's in the thought, doing his will. When many had received the light, they turned **31** to him. For the material ones were strangers, who didn't see his form or know him. For he came by means of fleshly form, and nothing could block his path, because incorruptibility can't be grasped. Moreover, he said new things while he spoke about what's in the Father's heart and brought out the complete Word. When the light spoke through his mouth, and by his voice gave birth to life, he gave them thought, wisdom, mercy, salvation, and the Spirit of power from the infinity and sweetness of the Father. He caused punishments and torments to cease, because they led astray into Error and bondage those who needed mercy. He dissolved and confounded them with knowledge. He became:

> a Way for those who were led astray,
> knowledge for those who were ignorant,
> a discovery for those who were searching,
> strength for those who were wavering, and
> purity for those who were impure.

The Parable of the Sheep

He's the shepherd who left behind the ninety- **32** nine sheep which weren't lost. He went and searched for the one which was lost. He rejoiced when he found it, because ninety-nine is a number expressed with the left hand. However, when the one is found, the numerical sum moves to the right hand. In this way, what needs the one – that is, the whole right hand – draws what it needs, takes it from the left hand, and moves it to the right, so the number becomes one hundred. This is a symbol of the sound of these numbers; this is the Father.

Even on the Sabbath, he worked for the sheep which he found fallen in the pit. He saved the life of the sheep, having brought it up from the pit, so that you may know in your hearts – you're children of the knowledge of the heart – what is the Sabbath, on which it isn't right for salvation to be idle, so that you may speak of the day which is above, which has no night, and of the light that doesn't set, because it's complete. Speak then from the heart, because you're the completed day, and the light that doesn't cease dwells within you. Speak of the Truth with those who search for it, and of knowledge with those who've sinned in their Error.

Doing the Father's Will

33 Strengthen the feet of those who stumble, and reach out to those who are sick. Feed those who are hungry, and give rest to those who are weary. Raise up those who want to arise, and awaken those who sleep, because you're the understanding that's unsheathed. If strength is like this, it becomes stronger.

Be concerned about yourselves. Don't be concerned about other things which you've rejected from yourselves. Don't return to eat your vomit. Don't be eaten by worms, because you've already shaken it off. Don't become a dwelling-place for the devil, because you've already brought him to naught. Don't strengthen your obstacles which are collapsing, as though you're a support. For the lawless one is nothing, to be treated more harshly than the just, doing his works among others.

Do then the Father's will, because you're from him. For the Father is sweet, and goodness is in his will. He knows what's yours, that you may find rest in them. For by the fruits they know what's yours, because the children of the Father **34** are his fragrance, since they're from the grace of his expression. Because of this, the Father loves his fragrance, and reveals it in every place. And when it mixes with matter, it gives his fragrance to the light, and in tranquility he causes it to rise above every form and every sound. For it's not the ears that smell the fragrance, but it's the Spirit that smells, and draws the fragrance to itself, and sinks down into the Father's fragrance. He shelters it, then, and takes it to the place from which it came, from the first fragrance which has grown cold. It's something in a soul-endowed delusion, like cold water sunk into loose earth. Those who see it think that it's just earth. Afterwards, it dissolves again. If a breath draws it, it becomes warm. So the fragrances which are cold are from the division. Because of this, faith came. It dissolved the division, and it brought the fullness that's warm with love, so that the cold may not return, but rather the unitary thought of completion.

Restoring what was Needed

This is the Word of the Gospel of the discovery of the fullness, which comes for those who are awaiting **35** the salvation which is coming from above. The hope for which they're waiting is waiting for those whose image is light with no shadow in it. If at that time the fullness comes, the need of matter doesn't come through the infinity of the Father, who comes to give time to the need – although no one can say that the incorruptible one will come like this. But the depth of the Father multiplied, and the thought of Error didn't exist with him. It's something that's fallen, which is easily set upright in the discovery of the one who's to come to what he'll return, because the return is called "repentance."

Because of this, incorruptibility breathed out. It followed after the one who sinned, so that they might rest, because forgiveness is what remains for the light in need, the Word of fullness. For the doctor hurries to the place where there's sickness, because that's what he (or she) wants to do. The one in need, then, doesn't hide it, because one (the doctor) has what they need. In this way the fullness, which has no need but fills the need, is what he **36** provided from himself to fill up what's needed, so that they might receive grace; because when they were in need, they didn't have grace. Because of this, a diminishing took place where there is no grace. When what was diminished was restored, what they needed was revealed as fullness. This is the discovery of the light of Truth which enlightened them, because it doesn't change.

Because of this, they spoke of Christ in their midst: "Seek, and those who were disturbed will receive a return – and he'll anoint them with ointment." The ointment is the mercy of the Father, who will have mercy on them. But those whom he anointed are those who have been completed, because full jars are the ones that are anointed. But when the anointing of one dissolves, it empties, and the cause of the need is the place where the ointment leaks, because a breath and its power draws it. But from the one who has no need, no seal is removed, nor is anything emptied, but what it needs is filled again by the Father, who's complete.

The Father's Paradise

He's good. He knows his plants, because he planted them in his paradise. Now his paradise is a place of rest. This **37** is the completion in the Father's thought, and these are the words of his meditation. Each of his words is the work of his one will in the revelation of his Word. When they were still in the depths of his thought, the Word – which was the first to come out – revealed them along with a mind that speaks the one Word in a silent grace. He was called "the Thought," since they were in it before being revealed. It happened, then, that he was the first to come out at the time when it pleased the one who wanted it. Now the Father rests in his will, and is pleased with it.

Nothing happens without him, nor does anything happen without the will of the Father, but his will is incomprehensible. His trace is the will, and no one can know him, nor does he exist for people to scrutinize so that they might grasp him, but when he wills, what he wills is this – even if the sight doesn't please them in any way before God – the will of the Father, because he knows the beginning of all of them, and their end, for in the end he'll greet them directly. Now the end is receiving knowledge of the one who's hidden; this is the Father, **38** from whom the beginning has come, and to whom all who've come out from him will return. They were revealed for the glory and the joy of his name.

The Father's Name

Now the name of the Father is the Son. He's the one who first gave a name to the one who comes out from him, who was himself, and he gave birth to him as a Son. He gave him his name which belonged to him. He's the one to whom everything around the Father belongs. The name and the Son are his. It's possible for him to be seen; the name, however, is invisible, because it alone is the mystery of the invisible which comes to ears that are filled completely with it by him. For indeed, the Father's name isn't spoken, but it's revealed through a Son.

In this way, then, the name is great. Who, then, will be able to utter a name for him, the great name, except him alone to whom the name belongs, and the children of the name, those in whom the Father's name rests, and who themselves, in turn, rest in his name? Since the Father is unbegotten, it's he alone who gave birth to him for himself as a name, before he had made the generations, so that the Father's name might be over their head as Lord, which is the **39** true name, confirmed in his command in complete power. For the name isn't from words and naming; the name, rather, is invisible.

He gave a name to him alone. He alone sees him, he alone having the power to give him a name, because whoever doesn't exist has no name. For what name will they give one who doesn't exist? But the one who exists, exists also with his name, and he alone knows it, and he's given a name to him alone. This is the Father; his name is the Son. He didn't hide it within, then, but it existed. The Son alone gave a name. The name, then, belongs to the Father, as the name of the Father is the beloved Son. Where, indeed, would he find a name, except from the Father?

But doubtless one will ask their neighbor, "Who is it who'll give a name to the one who existed before them, as if **40** offspring didn't receive a name from those who gave them birth?" First, then, it's right for us to consider what the name is. It's the true name, the name from the Father, because it's the proper name. So he didn't receive the name on loan, the way others do, according to the form in which each one will be produced. This, then, is the proper name. There's no one else who gave it to him. But he's unnameable, indescribable, until the time when he who's complete spoke of him alone. And it's he who has the power to speak his name and to see him.

So when it pleased him that his beloved name should be his Son, and he gave the name to him who came out from the depth, he disclosed his secrets, knowing that the Father is without evil. Because of this, he brought him out so that he might speak about the place, and his resting place from which he had come, **41** and to glorify the fullness, the greatness of his name, and the Father's sweetness.

The Place of Rest

Each one will speak about the place from which they came, and they'll hurry to return again to the place where they received their restoration to receive from the place where they were, receiving a taste from that place and receiving nourishment, receiving growth.

And their place of rest is their fullness. All that have emanated from the Father, then, are fullnesses, and the roots of all that have emanated from him are within the one who caused them all to grow. He gave them their destinies. Then each one was revealed, so that through their own thought […] for the place to which they send their thought is their root, which takes them up through all the heights, up to the Father. They embrace his head, which is rest for them, and they're grasped, approaching him, as though to say that they receive his expression by means of kisses. But they're not revealed **42** in this way, because they neither exalted themselves, nor wanted the Father's glory, nor did they think of him as trivial or harsh or wrathful; but he's without evil, unperturbed, and sweet. He knows every realm before they've come into existence, and he has no need to be instructed.

This is the way of those who possess something of the immeasurable greatness from above, as they wait for the complete one alone, who's a Mother for them. And they don't go down to Hades, nor do they have envy or groaning, nor death within them, but they rest in the one who rests, not striving nor twisting around in the search for Truth. But they themselves are the Truth, and the Father is within them, and they're in the Father, being complete. They're undivided from the truly good one. They don't need anything, but they rest, refreshed in the Spirit. And they'll listen to their root. They'll devote themselves to those things that they'll find in their root and not suffer loss to their soul. This is the place of the blessed; this is their place.

Conclusion

As for the others, then, may they know, where they're at, that it's not right **43** for me, having come to the place of rest, to say anything else, but I'll come to be in it, and will devote myself continually to the Father of all and the true brothers (and sisters), those upon whom the Father's love is emptied and in whose midst there is no need. They're the ones who are revealed in Truth; they exist in the true eternal life, and they speak of the light that's complete and that's filled with the Father's seed, and that's in his heart and in the fullness. His Spirit rejoices in it, and glorifies the one in whom it existed, because he's good. And his children are complete, and worthy of his name, because he's the Father. It's children like this that he loves.

The Gospel of Truth: The Mystical Gospel

Text Notes

Page 17: *"It happened in a deluding way."* Cf. Jörgen Magnusson, *Rethinking the Gospel of Truth: A Study of Its Eastern Valentinian Setting* (Uppsala University), 2006, p. 77, *contra* most translators, who tend to use *"creation"* or *"form"* for *plasma* instead of *"delusion."* Kendrick Grobel translates *"She was at work upon a molded figure"* in *The Gospel of Truth: A Valentinian Meditation on the Gospel* (Abingdon Press), 1960, p. 33 (but cf. p. 34); Attridge and MacRae translate *"it set about with a creation"* in James M. Robinson, ed., *The Coptic Gnostic Library: A Complete Edition of the Nag Hammadi Codices, Volume I* (Brill), 2000, p. 83 (but cf. the note in their commentary section later in the volume on p. 45); Marvin Meyer translates *"she assumed a fashioned figure"* in *The Nag Hammadi Scriptures* (HarperOne), 2007, p. 36; Celene Lillie translates *"She ... became a molded form"* in Hal Taussig, ed., *A New New Testament* (Houghton Mifflin Harcourt), 2013, p. 230; and Bentley Layton translates *"she took up residence in a modeled form"* in *The Gnostic Scriptures* (Doubleday), 1987, p. 253. The pronoun in the phrase is feminine (which could refer to *"Error,"* which is feminine in Coptic) but can also be rendered as *"it,"* as Coptic has no neuter gender. *"delusion of deceit."* Also following Magnusson (*op. cit.*, p. 94); cp. Grobel, *"deceitful figure"* (*op. cit.*, p. 44); Attridge and MacRae, *"creature of deceit"* (*op. cit.*, p. 83); Meyer, *"deceptive figure"* (*op. cit.*, p. 36); Lillie, *"molded forms are lies"* (*op. cit.*, p. 230); Layton, *"modeled form of deception"* (*op. cit.*, p. 253). *"disregard."* Grobel translates *"look with scorn"* (*op. cit.*, p. 46); Attridge and MacRae (*op. cit.*, p. 83), Meyer (*op. cit.*, p. 36), and Layton (*op. cit.*, p. 253) translate *"despise"*; but cf. Lillie, *op. cit.*, p. 230, and Magnusson, *op. cit.*, pp. 78, 79.

Page 18: *"thought."* The reconstruction is that of Magnusson, *op. cit.*, p. 81. *"This is the Gospel of the one they search for ... the Way is the Truth which he taught them."* Based on personal correspondence with Lance Jenott dated November 15, 2017.

Page 19: *"the Father's expressions."* Literally, "the forms of the Father's face."

Page 20: *"who'd been entrusted with."* Grobel (*op. cit.*, p. 62), Meyer (*op. cit.*, p. 38), and Layton (*op. cit.*, p. 255) translate *"those who believed in"*; Attridge and MacRae translate *"those who have believed in"* (*op. cit.*, p. 87); Lillie translates *"those who trust in"* (*op. cit.*, p. 231); but cf. Magnusson, *op. cit.*, pp. 137, 138.

Page 21: *"delusion."* Grobel translates *"figure"* (*op. cit.*, p. 74); Attridge and MacRae (*op. cit.*, p. 89) and Meyer (*op. cit.*, p. 35) translate *"creature"*; Lillie translates *"creatures"* (*op. cit.*, p. 231); Layton translates *"modeled form"* (*op. cit.*, p. 256); but cf. Magnusson, *op. cit.*, p. 100.

Page 22: *"He revealed his will as knowledge in harmony with all that emanated from him."* For clarity, this translation follows Lillie in omitting the preceding phrase which creates a logical incoherence: *"If his will hadn't come out from him."* It appears that either the author changed direction mid-sentence, or the scribe copying this text made an error.

Pages 23, 34, and 41: *"expression."* Literally, "form of face."

Page 34: *"delusion."* Grobel translates *"animate mold"* (*op. cit.*, p. 152); Attridge and MacRae (*op. cit.*, p. 105), Meyer (*op. cit.*, p. 44), and Lillie (*op. cit.*, p. 235) translate *"form"*; Layton translates *"modeled form"* (*op. cit.*, p. 261); but cf. Magnusson, *op. cit.*, p. 116.

Page 42: *"a Mother,"* following Meyer, *op. cit.*, p. 47 (but cf. n. 49); Lillie, *op. cit.*, p. 238 (but cf. note); Layton, *op. cit.*, p. 264. Alternatively, *"is there"*; cf. Grobel, *op. cit.*, p. 196; Attridge and MacRae, *op. cit.*, p. 117; Magnusson, *op. cit.*, p. 126.

Appendix B:
Two Versions of the Gospel of Truth

Chapter One noted continuity between the christology of the Gospel of Truth and fourth-century Christian tradition. More recently, scholars have begun to explore this connection by comparing the more complete copy of the Gospel of Truth in Codex I to the fragments in Codex XII.[1]

Though there may not be enough fragments in Codex XII to yield many points of meaningful comparison, there may be enough parallel passages to draw some tentative conclusions about theological differences. This may in turn provide hints about the evolution of the text.

According to Raoul Mortley, the Gospel's description of the Son's relationship to the Father on page 38 ("the name of the Father is the Son") implies a later revision of the text. He argues "that the Gospel of Truth was first written in about 170, subjected to revision and development in later periods, and that the Nag Hammadi text is a version which includes a response to the Arian debate, coming from the period 320 – 630 A.D."[2] The Athanasian-Arian debate was about the relationship between the Father and the Son. In an addendum to Mortley's essay, Michel Tardieu supports this argument by suggesting that the fragmented version in Codex XII, which lacks this passage, reflects an earlier version of the Gospel of Truth than the more complete version in Codex I.[3]

Yet, in a more recent essay, Katrine Brix raises more questions about the relationship between the two versions.[4] She writes, "it is difficult to determine which version is the earlier," and continues:

It is possible that these versions have undergone a journey of different turns before they ended up in NHC I and XII. But it is also possible that only one of them, possibly I,*3*, was transmitted over a longer period of time, while XII,*2* was produced on the basis of the version found in I,*3* at a later stage of development.[5]

In an article published in *Harvard Theological Review*, Geoffrey Smith argues that the fragments in Codex XII are an edited version of Codex I, rather than an earlier version of the text preserved in Codex I. Whereas he agrees that the Gospel of Truth "was likely composed sometime near the middle of the second century," he writes that "ancient readers of the *Gospel of Truth* would have associated many of its themes with the teachings of Origen and his supporters."[6]

Origen's critics believed that he "left dangerously thin the veil between Christ and humanity."[7] The Word was but one of many pre-existent souls, all of whom would be saved. Since Origen had fallen out of favor in the later church, "sometime in the fourth or fifth century an anonymous editor removed elements of the [Gospel of Truth] that could be read in support of the Origenist 'heresy' in order to produce a theologically-acceptable version of this compelling homily on the gospel."[8] For example, where page 37 of Codex I states that "the Word ... was the first to come out," page 60 of Codex XII describes "the Word, [who had] come."[9] By removing "the first," the scribe in Codex XII could have precluded the idea that there was a second, a third, a fourth, and so on. In other words, the editor may have intended to emphasize the uniqueness of the Son as compared to everyone else.

Whatever may be the relationship between these two Coptic versions, this debate suggests two likely things. First, ancient scribes revised the Gospel of Truth between the time of its composition in Greek in the second century and the time of its translation into Coptic in the fourth century. We can discern the same type of development in other early Gospels, like the fourth-

The Gospel of Truth: The Mystical Gospel

century Coptic Gospel of Thomas in Nag Hammadi Codex II, which differs from the third-century Greek fragments.[10]

Second, whatever their motivations, the fourth-century Egyptian scribes of the Nag Hammadi Codices revised the Gospel of Truth to bring its christology closer in line with mainstream discussions of fourth-century Christian theology.

This doesn't mean the original second-century Greek version was completely incompatible with later Christian theology, or in significant conflict with other second-century Christian texts; only that the Egyptian scribes composing later versions remained concerned about the theological conflicts of their own times.

Either way, the point is that the followers of Jesus who wrote and preserved this Gospel were as concerned about the validity of their faith as any other Jesus-followers in the first few centuries of the developing church.

The Gospel of Truth: The Mystical Gospel

Notes

Introduction

[1]Cf. Michel Malinine, Henri-Charles Puech, and Gilles Quispel, *Evangelium Veritatis* (Rascher Verlag), 1956; Michel Malinine, Henri-Charles Puech, Gilles Quispel, and Walter Till, *Evangelium Veritatis* (Rascher Verlag), 1961; Kendrick Grobel, *The Gospel of Truth: A Valentinian Meditation on the Gospel* (Abingdon Press), 1960.

[2]Bentley Layton, *The Gnostic Scriptures* (Doubleday), 1987, p. 250.

[3]Cf. Karen King, *What is Gnosticism?* (Harvard University Press), 2003, pp. 155, 156.

[4]Cf. Grobel, *op. cit.*, p. 17: "It has neither a title, nor an ascription of authorship, nor any colophon, but its first words are: 'The Gospel of Truth.' By its *incipit* it was known, as were many ancient books." Cf. also Harold W. Attridge and George W. MacRae in Robinson, James M., ed., *The Coptic Gnostic Library: A Complete Edition of the Nag Hammadi Codices, Volume I* (Brill), 2000, p. 65: "The third tractate of Codex I of the Nag Hammadi collection is, like the second and fifth tractates, untitled. It has come to be known in modern scholarship by its incipit, the 'Gospel of Truth.' It is not clear whether this incipit was designed to serve as a title in antiquity, but it is not improbable that it did originally function as the designation of the work, as did the incipits of the Gospel of Mark and the Revelation of John in the New Testament." But cf. Geoffrey Smith, "Anti-Origenist Redaction in the Fragments of the *Gospel of Truth* (NHC XII,2): Theological Controversy and

the Transmission of Early Christian Literature," *Harvard Theological Review*, 2017, Vol. 110, No. 1, p. 66: "Although Irenaeus does accuse some Valentinians of having a 'Gospel of Truth (*Veritatis Evangelium*)' as a fifth gospel in addition to the canonical four, we must resist the urge to identify uncritically this text with the *Gospel of Truth* known from Nag Hammadi, an untitled treatise given its title by modern editors." Cf. also the stronger statement by Katrine Brix, "Two Witnesses, One Valentinian Gospel? The *Gospel of Truth* in Nag Hammadi Codices I and XII," in *Snapshots of Evolving Traditions*, ed. by Liv Ingeborg Lied and Hugo Lundhaug (De Gruyter), 2017, p. 144: "The discovery of the *Gospel of Truth* is not the discovery of the text mentioned in the second century work of Irenaeus."

[5]Cf. Grobel, *op. cit.*, p. 26.

[6]Cf. Layton, *op. cit.*, p. 251; Jörgen Magnusson, *Rethinking the Gospel of Truth: A Study of Its Eastern Valentinian Setting* (Uppsala University), 2006, p. 181; cf. his full discussion on pp. 18-39.

[7]Cf. Layton, *op. cit.* On the other hand, although Valentinian authorship is entirely plausible, it has to be added that it remains conjectural. The author does refer to himself or herself in the text (cf. page 43), but nowhere identifies himself or herself. So although Valentinus' authorship may be surmised, it may be appropriate to leave some room for doubt.

[8]Cf. Layton, *op. cit.*, p. 217.

[9]"Likewise they allege that Valentinus was a hearer of Theudas. And he was the pupil of Paul" (*Strom.* VII.17). Alexander Roberts and James Donaldson, eds, *The Ante-Nicene Fathers: The Writings of the Fathers down to A.D. 325*, American Reprint of the Edinburgh Edition, Vol. II, ed. by A. Cleveland Coxe (Wm. B. Eerdmans Pub. Co.), reprint 1985, p. 555.

[10]Cf. Layton, *op. cit.*, p. 217.

[11]Tertullian, *Adv. Val.*, IV. Roberts and Donaldson, *op. cit.*, Vol. III, p. 505.

[12]After noting that Valentinus nearly became bishop of Rome, Tertullian continues with characteristic scathing commentary belying his extreme bias: "Being indignant, however, that another obtained the dignity by reason of a claim which confessorship had given him, he broke with the church of the true faith. Just like those (restless) spirits which, when roused by ambition, are usually inflamed with the desire of revenge, he applied himself with all his might to exterminate the truth" (*ibid.*). Valentinus would obviously have described it differently; and if he was indeed the author of the Gospel of Truth, his unwillingness to castigate his opponents in turn in his conclusion (page 43) testifies to his forgiveness and humility.

Chapter One

[1]Attridge and MacRae, *op. cit.*, p. 71.

[2]Conversation with Samuel Zinner on April 28, 2018.

[3]Cf. William F. Arndt and F. Wilbur Gingrich, *A Greek-English Lexicon of the New Testament and Other Early Christian Literature, Fourth Revised and Augmented Edition* (The University of Chicago Press), 1952, p. 513. Cynthia Bourgeault takes it much further, however. She builds on Marcus Borg's statement in *The Heart of Christianity: Rediscovering a Life of Faith* (HarperSanFrancisco), 2004, that "repentance in the New Testament has an additional nuance of meaning. The Greek roots of the word combine to mean 'go beyond the mind that you have.' Go beyond the mind that you have been given and have acquired. Go beyond the mind shaped by culture to the mind that you have 'in Christ'" (p. 180). In her book *The Wisdom Jesus: Transforming Heart and Mind – a New Perspective on Christ and His Message* (Shambhala), 2008, Bourgeault

writes, "The word literally breaks down into *meta* and *noia*, which, depending on how you translate *meta* (it can be either the preposition 'beyond' or the adjective 'large'), means 'go beyond the mind' or 'go into the large mind'" (p. 37), meaning a movement into "nondual knowingness of the heart which can see and live from the perspective of wholeness" (p. 41). But I feel ambivalent about this definition, at best, since "large" is not a potential meaning of *meta*.

[4] Cf. Grobel, *op. cit.*, pp. 161, 163; Elliot R. Wolfson, "Inscribed in the Book of the Living: *Gospel of Truth* and Jewish Christology," *Journal for the Study of Judaism*, 2007, Vol. 38, p. 249.

[5] Grobel, *op. cit.*, p. 181.

[6] Attridge and MacRae, *op. cit.*, *Notes*, pp. 120-121.

[7] Wolfson, *op. cit.*, pp. 249, 250; cf. also Charles A. Gieschen, "The Divine Name in Ante-Nicene Christology," *Vigiliae Christianae*, Vol. 57, No. 2, pp. 115-158. Gieschen goes on to compare "the name" in the Gospel of Truth (NHC I, *3*, 38.7-24) with "the name" in the Gospel of Philip (NHC II, *3*, 53.5-13): "Both of these texts testify to the 'hidden name' tradition and both evince the Jewish tradition that the Divine Name is not spoken. The *Gospel of Philip*, however, appears to reflect older Jewish-Christian adoptionist Christology in the mention of 'put on himself the Name of the Father' (*i.e.*, the Son's divine nature was imparted to Jesus at his baptism). The *Gospel of Truth* takes its Name Christology further than the *Gospel of Philip*: The Son is not only *given* the Name of the Father; he *is* the hypostasized Name of the Father" (*ibid.*, p. 155).

[8] From Roberts and Donaldson, *op. cit.*, Vol. II, ed. by A. Cleveland Coxe (Wm. B. Eerdmans Pub. Co.), reprint 1985.

[9] Cf. Grobel, *op. cit.*, p. 39; Attridge and MacRae, *op. cit.*, *Notes*, pp. 42, 43.

[10]Cf. Rev. 3:5; 13:8; 17:8; 20:12, 15; 21:27.

[11]Correspondence with Samuel Zinner dated May 3, 2018.

[12]Zinner elaborates: "The book is living because the constellation at work here is: the Torah as tree of life (Prov. 3), the cross as tree of life = Torah. The Torah is living because personified as a living person (Sirach 24; Baruch 3-4), Lady Wisdom. This helps explain why Jesus is the mother; he is the book who is the Torah who is Lady Wisdom, described as a mother in Prov. and Sirach. ... 'as long as that book had not appeared.' Here we see the language of Baruch 3:37, 'Afterward she appeared upon earth and lived among [humans],' and 4:1, 'She is the book of the commandments of God, and the law that endures forever. All who hold her fast will live...' I think Baruch 3-4 is a direct literary source, together with Sirach 24, for the living book passages in Gos Tr. ... To sum up, while Gos Tr may not be 'Jewish Christian,' it has somehow inherited some Jewish-based traditions" *(ibid)*.

[13]Cf. *Bereshit Rabbah* 17:5; Daniel C. Matt, *The Essential Kabbalah: The Heart of Jewish Mysticism* (HarperSanFrancisco), 1995, p. 145.

[14]Though cf. the Text Note on page 42 in Appendix A.

[15]Correspondence with Samuel Zinner dated April 28, 2018.

[16]Cf. Attridge and MacRae, *op. cit., Notes*, pp. 43, 44.

[17]Cf. Mattison, *The Gospel of Judas: The Sarcastic Gospel* (Createspace), 2014, p. 27.

[18]Magnusson, *op. cit.*, p. 87.

[19]Cf. Magnusson, *op. cit.*, p. 90: "Error appears on the one hand as a frightening monster, and on the other as nothing, 17.21b-27, 26.18-27."

[20]*Ibid.*, pp. 91, 92. Cf. also his comment on p. 90 that "the tendency of page 17 in the GospTruth is a demythologizing one."

[21]Correspondence dated April 29, 2018.

[22]Cf. Magnusson, *op. cit.*, p. 88.

[23]Correspondence with Samuel Zinner dated May 3, 2018.

[24]King, *op. cit.*, p. 193.

[25]Grobel, *op. cit.*, p. 103.

[26]Magnusson, *op. cit.*, pp. 173, 174.

[27]Cf. Mattison, *The Gospel of Philip: The Divine Mysteries of Marriage and Rebirth* (CreateSpace), 2017, pp. 15, 19.

[28]Could this passage in the Gospel of Truth also shed light on an obscure passage in the Gospel of Thomas? Saying 97 in Thomas presents a parable about a broken jar, followed in Saying 98 by a parable about an assassin practicing with a sword. (Samuel Zinner mentioned this potential connection in conversation on April 28, 2018.)

[29]David A. Cooper, *God is a Verb: Kabbalah and the Practice of Jewish Mysticism* (Riverhead Books), 1997, p. 29.

[30]If it seems anachronistic to propose an interpretation of a second- or fourth-century text in light of much later kabbalah, one may consider other precursors to the Shattering of the Vessels, as in 2 Enoch; cf. Andrei Orlov, "Adoil Outside the Cosmos: God Before and After Creation in the Enochic Tradition," in April D. De Conick and Grant Adamson, eds., *Histories Of The Hidden God: Concealment And Revelation In Western Gnostic, Esoteric, And Mystical Traditions* (Acumen Publishing), 2013, pp. 30-57.

[31]Cf. Mattison, *Philip*, pp. 31, 32.

Chapter Three

[1]Roberts and Donaldson, *op. cit.*, p. 315.

[2]*Adv. Haer.* I.XI.1; Roberts and Donaldson, *op. cit.*, p. 332. Some scholars, like Layton *(op. cit.)*, narrowly define the "Gnostic" movement itself (which Irenaeus says influenced Valentinus) as "Sethian Gnosticism." (For a list of "Sethian" texts, cf. Mattison, *Judas*, p. 68, n. 9.) They then regard "Valentinian Gnosticism" as a unique Christian version (or development) of "Sethian Gnosticism" (but cf. King, *op. cit.*, pp. 162, 163). The following texts in the Nag Hammadi Library have been identified as "Valentinian": The Prayer of the Apostle Paul (NHC I, *1*), The Gospel of Truth (NHC I, *3*; XII, *2*), The Treatise on the Resurrection (NHC I, *4*), The Tripartate Tractate (NHC I, *5*), The Gospel of Philip (NHC II, *3*), The Interpretation of Knowledge (NHC XI, *1*), and A Valentinian Exposition (NHC XI, *2*). Other candidates include The First Apocalypse of James (NHC V, *3*; cf. TC *2*), The Second Apocalypse of James (NHC V, *4*), and The Letter of Peter to Philip (NHC VIII, *2*; cf. TC *1*). Cf. Meyer, *op. cit.*, p. 791; Ismo Dunderberg, "The School of Valentinus," in Antti Marjanen, ed., *A Companion to Second-Century Christian 'Heretics'* (Brill), 2008, p. 84; Michel Desjardins, "The Sources for Valentinian Gnosticism: A Question of Methodology," *Vigiliae Christianae*, 1986, Vol. 40, p. 342.

[3]Cf. Mattison, *Judas*, p. 40.

[4]Cf. Roberts and Donaldson, *op. cit.*, pp. 312, 313: "The full title of the principal work of Irenaeus, as given by Eusebius (*Hist. Eccl.*, v. 7), and indicated frequently by the author himself, was *A Refutation and Subversion of Knowledge falsely so called*, but it is generally referred to under the shorter title, *Against Heresies*."

[5]For this, and much of what follows, cf. Mattison, *Judas*, p. 41.

[6] Cf. King, *op. cit.*; Michael Allen Williams, *Rethinking "Gnosticism": An Argument for Dismantling a Dubious Category* (Princeton University Press), 1996.

[7] Cf. Mattison, *Judas*, p. 42. Interestingly, one of the Nag Hammadi tractates, the Testimony of Truth, even criticizes Valentinus (cf. NHC IX, *3*, 56.1, 5).

[8] King, *op. cit.*, p. 192.

[9] Determining what constitutes "Valentinianism" itself actually involves a methodological dilemma. First, we lack first-hand evidence that either Valentinus or those who followed in his tradition even described themselves as "Valentinian." Second, unlike "Sethian" texts which scholars group together based on similar content (cf. Mattison, *Judas*, p. 44), "Valentininan" texts are primarily identified based on their similarity to the beliefs attributed to specific Valentinian teachers in the polemical works of the "church fathers." Consequently, much depends on how effectively we can critically read (and read between the lines of) Valentinus' critics. Cf. Desjardins, *op. cit.*, pp. 342-347.

[10] Though taking the position that Valentinianism was a school, Ismo Dunderberg agrees that Valentinians were still part of the church: "Thus far, I have argued, concurring with many other scholars, that Valentinians are best understood in the setting of a school. I assume that this explanation also applies to the Valentinians in Rome. The representatives of this school did not drift apart from the ordinary (whatever that may mean in the context of second-century Rome) Christian church. On the contrary, the Valentinian Florinus was able to become a member of church hierarchy still at the end of the second century CE." Dunderberg, *op. cit.*, p. 169. Dunderberg goes on to argue, however, that the Marcosians were an exception, having developed a unique "'Valentinian' church" (p. 173).

[11]Grobel, *op. cit.*, p. 56; but on p. 57, n. 86, he wonders whether the phrase may describe a synagogue.

[12]Attridge and MacRae, *op. cit.*, p. 87.

[13]Layton, *op. cit.*, p. 254.

[14]Meyer, *op. cit.*, p. 37.

[15]*A New New Testament*, *op. cit.*, p. 231.

[16]Geoffrey S. Smith, *Guilt by Association: Heresy Catalogues in Early Christianity* (Oxford University Press), 2014 pp. 165, 166.

[17]Cf. n. 9 above.

Appendix B

[1]Initially, scholars considered the version in Codex XII too fragmentary to allow any meaningful comparison; cf. Geoffrey Smith, *Anti-Origenist Redaction*, pp. 49, 50.

[2]Raoul Mortley, "The Name of the Father is the Son," in Richard T. Wallis, ed., *Neoplatonism and Gnosticism* (Sate of University New York Press), 1992, p. 249.

[3]*Ibid.*, pp. 249, 250.

[4]Cf. Brix, *op. cit.*

[5]*Ibid.*, p. 144.

[6]Smith, *op. cit.*, p. 48.

[7]*Ibid.*, p. 65.

[8]*Ibid.*, p. 49.

[9]*Ibid.*, p. 63. For additional examples, cf. the entire section in pp. 58-65.

[10]Cf. Mark M. Mattison, *The Gospel of Thomas: A New Translation for Spiritual Seekers* (CreateSpace), 2015, p. 20.

Bibliography

The Facsimile Edition of the Nag Hammadi Codices: Codex I (Brill), 1977

Arndt, William F. and Gingrich, F. Wilbur, *A Greek-English Lexicon of the New Testament and Other Early Christian Literature, Fourth Revised and Augmented Edition* (The University of Chicago Press), 1952

Borg, Marcus J., *The Heart of Christianity: Rediscovering a Life of Faith* (HarperSanFrancisco), 2003

Bourgeault, Cynthia, *The Wisdom Jesus: Transforming Heart and Mind – a New Perspective on Christ and His Message* (Shambhala), 2008

Brix, Katrine, "Two Witnesses, One Valentinian Gospel? The *Gospel of Truth* in Nag Hammadi Codices I and XII," in Liv Ingeborg Lied and Hugo Lundhaug, eds., *Snapshots of Evolving Traditions,* (De Gruyter), 2017, pp. 126-145

Cooper, David A., *God is a Verb: Kabbalah and the Practice of Jewish Mysticism* (Riverhead Books), 1997

Desjardins, Michel, "The Sources for Valentinian Gnosticism: A Question of Methodology," *Vigiliae Christianae,* 1986, Vol. 40, pp. 342-347

Dunderberg, Ismo, "The School of Valentinus," in Antti Marjanen, ed., *A Companion to Second-Century Christian 'Heretics'* (Brill), 2008

Gieschen, Charles A., "The Divine Name in Ante-Nicene Christology," *Vigiliae Christianae*, Vol. 57, No. 2, pp. 115-158

Grobel, Kendrick, *The Gospel of Truth: A Valentinian Meditation on the Gospel* (Abingdon Press), 1960

King, Karen, *What is Gnosticism?* (Harvard University Press), 2003

Layton, Bentley, *The Gnostic Scriptures* (Doubleday), 1987

Magnusson, Jörgen, *Rethinking the Gospel of Truth: A Study of Its Eastern Valentinian Setting* (Uppsala University), 2006

Malinine, Michel, Puech, Henri-Charles, and Quispel, Gilles, *Evangelium Veritatis* (Rascher Verlag), 1956

Malinine, Michel, Puech, Henri-Charles, Quispel, Gilles, and Till, Walter, *Evangelium Veritatis* (Rascher Verlag), 1961

Matt, Daniel C., *The Essential Kabbalah: The Heart of Jewish Mysticism* (HarperSanFrancisco), 1995

Mattison, Mark M., *The Gospel of Judas: The Sarcastic Gospel* (CreateSpace), 2014

Mattison, Mark M., *The Gospel of Mary: A Fresh Translation and Holistic Approach* (CreateSpace), 2013

Mattison, Mark M., *The Gospel of Philip: The Divine Mysteries of Marriage and Rebirth* (CreateSpace), 2017

Mattison, Mark M., *The Gospel of Thomas: A New Translation for Spiritual Seekers* (CreateSpace), 2015

Meyer, Marvin, ed., *The Nag Hammadi Scriptures* (HarperOne), 2007

Mortley, Raoul, "The Name of the Father is the Son," in Richard T. Wallis, ed., *Neoplatonism and Gnosticism* (State of University New York Press), 1992, pp. 239-252

Orlov, Andrei, "Adoil Outside the Cosmos: God Before and After Creation in the Enochic Tradition," in April D. De Conick and Grant Adamson, eds., *Histories Of The Hidden God: Concealment And Revelation In Western Gnostic, Esoteric, And Mystical Traditions* (Acumen Publishing), 2013, pp. 30-57

Roberts, Alexander, and Donaldson, James, eds., *The Ante-Nicene Fathers: The Writings of the Fathers down to A.D. 325*, American Reprint of the Edinburgh Edition, ed. by Cleveland Coxe (Wm. B. Eerdmans Pub. Co.), 10 volumes, reprint 1985

Robinson, James M., ed., *The Coptic Gnostic Library: A Complete Edition of the Nag Hammadi Codices, Volume I* (Brill), 2000

Robinson, James M., ed., *The Nag Hammadi Library in English*, 4th rev. ed. (Brill), 1996

Smith, Geoffrey, "Anti-Origenist Redaction in the Fragments of the *Gospel of Truth* (NHC XII,2): Theological Controversy and the Transmission of Early Christian Literature," *Harvard Theological Review* (2017), Vol. 110, No. 1, pp. 46-74

Smith, Geoffrey S., *Guilt by Association: Heresy Catalogues in Early Christianity* (Oxford University Press), 2014

Taussig, Hal, ed., *A New New Testament* (Houghton Mifflin Harcourt), 2013

Williams, Michael Allen, *Rethinking "Gnosticism": An Argument for Dismantling a Dubious Category* (Princeton University Press), 1996

Wolfson, Elliot R., "Inscribed in the Book of the Living: *Gospel of Truth* and Jewish Christology," *Journal for the Study of Judaism*, 2007, Vol. 38, pp. 234-271

Made in the USA
Lexington, KY
02 July 2019